Dark Side
of the Light

Dark Side
of the Light

SLAVERY AND THE FRENCH ENLIGHTENMENT

Louis Sala-Molins

*Translated and with an Introduction
by John Conteh-Morgan*

University of Minnesota Press
Minneapolis | London

Published by the University of Minnesota Press
111 Third Avenue South, Suite 290
Minneapolis, MN 55401-2520
http://www.upress.umn.edu

Printed in the United States of America on acid-free paper

Library of Congress Cataloging-in-Publication Data

Sala-Molins, Louis.
    [Misères des Lumières. English]
    Dark side of the light : slavery and the French Enlightenment / Louis Sala-Molins ; translated and with an introduction by John Conteh-Morgan.
       p.   cm.
    Includes bibliographical references (p.   ) and index.
    ISBN 0-8166-4389-X (hc : alk. paper) — ISBN 0-8166-4388-1 (pb : alk. paper)
      1. Slavery—France—Colonies—America—History—18th century.
  2. West Indies, French—Race relations—History—18th century.
  3. Abolitionists—France—History—18th century.   4. Enlightenment—France.   I. Title.
    HT1108.Z5S2513 2006
    306.3'62094409033—dc22

                                   2005028446

12 11 10 09 08 07 06   10 9 8 7 6 5 4 3 2 1

Contents

The Color of the Enlightenment

Contexts: Memory and Forgetting

In recent years, specifically since the last decade of the twentieth century, France has been going through a period of painful national debate about its official role in a number of key historical events. Of course, as Derrida observes in *Sur parole: Instantanés philosophiques* (1999, 123–45)—his reflections on pardon, forgiveness, and memory in the context of post-apartheid South Africa—such debates and acts of soul searching and the national work of memory to which they have sometimes given rise are not limited to France: "Today these scenes are taking place across the face of the earth," he writes, "with heads of state asking forgiveness from specific communities or other states in Europe and the entire world" (128). In the case of France, the first such recent public debate is the one concerning the deportation to their death of French Jews during the Vichy regime. After several decades of silence about these events, a period during which the national narrative about World War II spoke only the language of resistance (even though historians were already quietly challenging it [Paxton 1972]), the French state through its president admitted in 1995 to the moral necessity of recognizing its complicity in the tragic events of that period (Jelen 2002).

A second and no less painful event that France has (again) been confronting is the Algerian War and specifically the events of 1961, when many Algerians lost their lives in Paris in a demonstration that was brutally broken up by the police.[1] Never far from the surface of the national consciousness, the wounds of this period were reopened with the publication of books in which some members of the military of the period admitted to the widespread use of state-sanctioned torture and murder.[2] Although no recognition of responsibility by the French government has been registered, the city of Paris in 2001 took what has been seen as a tentative step in this direction with the commemoration of a plaque to the memory of the Algerian victims of the events of 1961 (see Jelen 2002).

The event and the act of collective introspection related to it most relevant to the present book concern the role of France in an enterprise that lasted some four hundred years and was abolished over a century ago: the slave trade and French Caribbean and Indian Ocean plantation slavery. While the late-twentieth-century French national debate on this issue may not have attained the scope or displayed the rawness of emotion associated with those issues mentioned above, it led to a significant result: the enactment into law by the French National Assembly in May 2001, after two years of debate, of the Taubira-Delannon Bill, so named after the deputy (for French Guyana) who introduced it in parliament.[3] Article 1 of this law declares:

> The French Republic acknowledges that the Atlantic and
> Indian Ocean slave trade on the one hand, and slavery on
> the other, perpetrated from the fifteenth century in the

Americas, the Caribbean, the Indian Ocean and in Europe, against African, Amerindian, Malagasy and Indian peoples constitute a crime against humanity. (Loi Taubira-Delannon N° 2001-434, in *Le Journal Officiel,* May 21 2001, 8175)[4]

The law further acknowledges, in Articles 2 and 4, the need to create spaces of memory in the French collective imagination through the introduction to the school history curriculum of courses on slavery, and the commemoration by local communities across France of a Slavery Remembrance Day, this to "ensure that the memory of this crime lives forever in future generations" (Article 4).

I have opened my introduction to *Dark Side of the Light: Slavery and the French Enlightenment* with these issues of memory and commemoration first to situate the book in the moral and political climate of opinion of the 1990s, when it was written and which it reflects in important ways. Second, I want to draw attention to the important contribution, academic as well as activist, made by Louis Sala-Molins, the book's author, in creating this climate and in shaping and raising public awareness of the issues through his books (1987, 1992a, 1992b), interviews (2002a), magazine and newspaper articles (1999, 2002b), and various public interventions (2000). Not only were some of his arguments and formulations used in the parliamentary debates on the question—sometimes literally even if not always with proper attribution, he wryly observed (1987, x, n. 1)—he was the rare if not the only French academic invited, in March 2000, to testify before the French senate on the issue.[5]

A Frenchman of Catalonian roots, Sala-Molins, now an emeritus, was a professor of political philosophy in various universities including the Sorbonne, where he held the chair vacated by Vladimir Jankélévitch, and Toulouse-Le-Mirail. He came to public attention, after an early career teaching and researching medieval philosophers and the Inquisition, with the publication in 1987 of his edition of *Le Code noir ou le calvaire de Canaan,* the body of laws, statutes, and decrees that codified and regulated the practice of French Caribbean slavery and was promulgated in 1685 under Louis XIV. Sala-Molins's book (now in its seventh edition) both reproduces and meticulously analyzes each of the sixty articles of the *Code noir* (last edited in 1788), bringing out the inconsistencies in and between articles, providing sources for the articles in Roman law, canon law, and the earlier Spanish Black Code, which he also edited (1992b), and situating the document in its appropriate historical, religious, and ideological contexts.

"The most monstrous legal document of modern times," writes Sala-Molins from his natural rights perspective (1987, 9), the *Code noir* manages the conceptual feat of yoking together what Rousseau was later to qualify as meaningless and mutually exclusive notions—"slavery" and "right."[6] It condemns the black African slave to legal and political nonexistence, declares her "chattel" (*meuble*) (Article 44),[7] and legitimizes her enslavement not in economic terms but—we shall come back to this issue—as a necessary process of redemption of her soul.[8]

To the ordinary French citizen whose memory of France's role in modern slavery is shaped by a celebratory nationalist discourse (at full throttle during the 1989 bicentennial of the Revolution, as we shall see later)[9] and marked by a few momentous dates and heroic names—1793 and 1794 (the earliest attempts at abolition by Sonthonax and the Convention respectively), 1848, when slavery was definitively abolished by Schoelcher, and by the great critique of slavery by such Enlightenment thinkers and abolitionists as Condorcet, Montesquieu, the abbés Raynal and Grégoire—the disinterment of a text, *Le Code noir,* that establishes French state involvement in the institutionalization and legalization of slavery came as an immense surprise.[10] But an even greater surprise, even for Sala-Molins, was the realization that this document and, with it, slavery remained in force for 163 years, surviving the ancien régime, the Enlightenment and Revolution, and the Empire to be finally and definitively repealed only during the Second Republic. That it survived the ancien régime is perhaps to be expected. What was less expected, however, is that it also did (and more) the French Enlightenment. The *Code noir* actually found understanding with the Enlightenment's many leading thinkers—tearful understanding is what Condorcet would claim in his *Réflexions sur l'esclavage des nègres* (1788) but understanding all the same—that is, when they were not quite simply silent on it. And this, notwithstanding their universalist doctrine of rights. In short, then, Sala-Molins was able to bring to light the fact that the Enlightenment, especially when read in *the context of and side by side with* the *Code noir,* is not all light and radiance as traditionally presented but also night and darkness, not all insight but also blindness. While the Enlightenment's core values are *abstractly* antithetical to all that the *Code noir* symbolized, it nonetheless managed to find accommodation with that body of laws and, as in the case of Montesquieu, to suggest ways of improving the lot of the slave that were worse than was contained in the *Code noir* (see Sala-Molins 1987, 230–37). It proclaimed the inalienability of human rights but excluded to various degrees and for different reasons entire categories of humans (for example, Jews, women, slaves) from the purview of their applicability.

It is this dark side of the French Enlightenment as it specifically relates to slavery that the author, building on earlier work in the field,[11] sought to bring to wider public knowledge in *Le Code noir ou le calvaire de Canaan* (1987). It is also to this dark side that he returns five years later in his 1992 book *Dark Side of the Light: Slavery and the French Enlightenment* (in the original French, *Les Misères des Lumières: Sous la raison, l'outrage*). Because the 1992 book is a spin-off from the 1987 volume and presupposes to be properly appreciated familiarity with the detailed arguments of that volume, I will make frequent references to some of those arguments in this introduction.

It is obviously impossible within the framework of a short translator's introduction to fully convey the substance of Sala-Molins's 1992 book. In what follows, I propose to (1) comment on its reading strategies and form and their significance, (2) provide the reader with a few concrete examples of the paradoxes and contradictions in the Enlightenment texts it examines, (3) discuss the reasons the author advances to explain these problems, (4) raise a few possible objections to his arguments, and (5) conclude by relating *Dark Side of the Light* to the 1989 French bicentennial celebrations of the Revolution, an event that Sala-Molins holds in constant parallel to the Enlightenment, that frames his entire discussion of the Enlightenment, and that enables him to link it to a consideration of issues in contemporary French politics.

The Margin Reads Back

Dark Side of the Light is an unconventional and in many respects a polemical reading of French Enlightenment thinking on the problem of slavery.[12] It is unconventional in two respects. The first is in its oppositional or "off-center" reading of some of the founding texts of modernity. It adopts in its approach to them the perspective from "below"—not just in class and gender but also in racial terms—the perspective of those in the outermost margins of eighteenth-century French life, the "barefooted, the starving, the slaves" (1992a, chapter 2). Although Sala-Molins does not use the word *postcolonial* itself, his reading practice can easily be qualified as such.[13] It is postcolonial in the way it foregrounds in its approach to canonical Enlightenment texts and thinkers the awkwardly material and often repressed issues (in polite society as in scholarship) of race, plantation slavery, and colonial domination, issues that were a "major concern," as Malick Ghachem has recently recalled, "of the *philosophes* and their nineteenth century successors" (2000, 8).

Referring, for example, to the focus of his Sorbonne lectures on Montesquieu, Sala-Molins declares, "I was not interested . . . in the marvels of the separation of powers, whose transcendent importance in the history of ideas and institutions is well known. I spent time instead showing the ease with which one could catch in the same man, at the same time, and in the same texts, so much generosity of spirit . . . and so much money-grubbing insolence in justifying for the France of his time the continuation of the practice of Roman-like slavery" (1992a, chapter 2). A focus such as this is one that mainstream scholarship, concentrating on the loftily philosophical or the *geographically and ethnically European,* often deems irrelevant or at best marginal to the concerns of the age. As Paul Gilroy observes, "interest in the social and political subordination of blacks and other non-European peoples does not generally feature in contemporary debates around the philosophical, ideological, or cultural content and consequences of modernity" (1993, 44). And yet such subordination should be a part of contemporary debate, contends Sala-Molins, because insofar as that subordination is based on a theory of "man," the "human" and the "inhuman," on an anthropology in other words (more on this later), it is in fact key, and not marginal, to a fuller understanding of the French Enlightenment: "the crucial test for the Enlightenment," he writes, "is the slave trade and slavery. To interpret [it] without them is to play the game of the Enlightenment: it is tantamount to limiting universal philanthropy to one's neighborhood" (1992a, preface).

A second unconventional feature of *Dark Side of the Light* is its form. The author's decision to read and understand the center from its occluded and, in this case, literally enslaved margins finds materialization in his choice of form. He eschews the conventions of traditional academic writing much in evidence in, for example, the critical apparatus of *Le Code noir.* In *Dark Side of the Light,* he resorts instead to the techniques of the creative writer, interspersing his expository prose with scenes of dialogue between an imaginary slave and various Enlightenment thinkers. In other words, the "I" in the book refers at times to the author-historian of ideas, at other times to the slave, at other times to the slaver, and at other times still to the author as fictional interlocutor of the imaginary slave. The result is a book of striking originality of form and styles in which the high and the low, the slave and the philosopher, the detached scholar and the crusading pamphleteer, the disembodied language of learned discourse and the somatic language of the slave's suffering body all mix.

Now, readers used to the standard scholarly monograph might find the book's sometimes graphic, denunciatory, and on occasion inflammatory language, its tendency to cross the line between analysis and activism, unfortunate, perhaps excessive, very probably disconcerting. What should be remembered, however, is that the use of this language is deliberate. To Sala-Molins, discussions of slavery cannot be just conceptual, for slavery was also (need it be said) an experience of physical and existential dereliction, and *that* needs to be conveyed, if only to express outrage and to give a sense of moral and political urgency to the discussion. In this sense he falls squarely within a certain eighteenth-century tradition of the socially and politically committed writer—the Voltaire of the Calas affair, for example, to whom he refers admiringly in his book (1992a, chapter 2). Equally disconcerting but also very deliberate is the device of making the slave—the great absentee in all the learned discussions on his fate—intervene throughout the book. This is part of Sala-Molins's overall project of restoring the slave's humanity by giving him initiative and voice. Once the decision to make the slave speak is made, his speech is subject to the constraints of the genre if he is to sound credible. Because he is uneducated, brutalized, and angry, he has to speak in character to carry literary conviction, and thus he must use the language of (feigned) naïveté, sarcasm and irony, and sometimes invective. The issues discussed are serious, but the tone the author/slave adopts (also like the eighteenth-century writers he critiques) is deflationary, the tone of derision.

It may be tempting at this point to see in *Dark Side of the Light* nothing more than a contemporary instance of what, presumably in fit of irritation at what he sees as the besmirching of a great movement, a distinguished historian has called "the old accusations" (Darnton 1997, 36) against the Enlightenment, "accusations" that he attributes to those in the camp of the "postmodernists and anti-westernizers" (35). But to view the book this way would be to seriously misread it, for Sala-Molins clearly does not reject the French Enlightenment even if he is aware of its limitations. On the contrary, he is strongly committed to what he sees as its emancipatory values: reason, justice, universalism, and equality. His critique, in other words, is not directed at those core values per se, which it has been argued is the case, for example, with Max Horkheimer and Theodor Adorno in *Dialectic of Enlightenment* ([1947] 2000), and Michel Foucault (Racevskis, 1998, 65–87; Bronner 1995), but rather at the Enlightenment's failure to extend these values to apply to *all* human beings at all times, in other words, to be true to itself by being truly and fully universal. Put differently, for Sala-Molins, the universalizable normative claims of the Enlightenment (to human equality, for example), far from being repressive of the particular—a well-known criticism by postmodernists— are an indispensable reference point for any meaningful contestation of injustice.[14] It is precisely because the French Enlightenment was not universalist enough on the question of slavery, contends the author, that it betrayed its promise and thus remained an incomplete project. Nowhere is this more in evidence to him than in the text to which he devotes most of the book's first of three chapters: Condorcet's *Réflexions sur l'esclavage des nègres* (1788), a text that Condorcet wrote under the pseudonym M. Schwartz (Mr. Negro in German), presumably, Sala-Molins suggests, to identify with the subjects of its contents.

Paradoxes and Contradictions

The picture of Condorcet's *Réflexions* that emerges from Sala-Molins's text is of a thought deeply entangled in intellectual contradiction. Sala-Molins gives samples of the positive term of this contradiction: *Réflexions*'s uncompromising condemnation of slavery. "Any polity" Condorcet writes, "where general peace is secured through the violation of the rights of its citizens or its foreigners ceases to be a society of human beings to become a den of thieves" (quoted in Sala-Molins 1992a, chapter 1). Sala-Molins also points admiringly to such facts as the French thinker's demolition of the idea of natural or voluntary slavery, and to his dismissal as pure fabrication of the pro-slavery argument that sees in slavery a humanitarian act that saves the lives of war captives from certain death. Nowhere in the world, Condorcet argues, are prisoners systematically put to death. But even if they were, "it's no less a crime to buy [them] if it's to re-sell [them] or reduce [them] to slavery" (1788, 5). "The crime" to him is even worse for the colonists in the French Caribbean islands, who could not claim to be rescuing their enslaved from certain death, since these were born and raised on the plantation (see Condorcet 1788: 7).

But *Réflexions,* Sala-Molins is quick to point out, is not all generosity of spirit, the only aspect often presented in support of its author's abolitionism.[15] It also has truck with what ought to be "nonnegotiable, [and] cheapens what it adores," Sala-Molins remarks (1992a, chapter 1). In support of this view, he emphasizes Condorcet's opposition to the elevation of the slave to the realm of the human through the *immediate* and effective recognition of her rights: "The slaves in the European colonies have become incapable of carrying out normal human functions," asserts Condorcet, and like "children, madmen and idiots," should therefore be deemed to have "lost their rights or as not having acquired them" (quoted in Sala-Molins 1992a, chapter 1). He at best concedes to them what Sala-Molins (1992a, chapter 1), borrowing the vocabulary of the sixteenth-century Spanish theologian Bartolomé Las Casas, calls "monastic" and "domestic" sovereignty (the sovereignty to exercise dominion over oneself and one's household, respectively), but not political sovereignty, the right to be a member of civil society and participate in the deliberations of the body politic.[16] Such a right presupposes a faculty of the "will," "rationality," and "personhood," attributes that Condorcet like the *Code noir* denies the slave.[17] He may be physically human, but the slave is not a "person,"[18] or what in the French language of the age was known as an "accomplished man."

So, in spite of his lofty enunciation of principles, Condorcet, the many times president of the abolitionist 1788 Society of the Friends of Blacks, finds himself unable to apply those principles. Instead of calling for immediate abolition, he equivocates and compromises, only to opt (in the chapter "Des moyens de détruire l'esclavage des nègres par degrés" [On the Ways of Destroying Slavery in Stages]) for a formula of phased emancipation according to which (to bring out a few of its proposals) children born into slavery are emancipated only at thirty-five; those who are fifteen at the time of his suggestions, at forty; and those above fifteen only when they are fifty, and so on (Sala-Molins 1992a, chapter 1; Condorcet, 1788, 38–52). Condorcet further goes on to recommend (1788, 67–70) as compensation to those religious and ethnic minorities—Jews and Protestants—whose civic and political rights had been severely curtailed as a result of the 1685 revocation of the Edict of Nantes, their resettlement in Haiti and commercial involvement in slavery.

Even allowing for Condorcet's political evolution into a radical abolitionist on the eve of the Revolution, Sala-Molins still detects ambiguity in his speech to the Convention when he spoke, with fellow Society of Blacks member the Jansenist abbé Grégoire, against the idea of admitting as deputies of the free nation into the Convention members of Haiti's white slave-owning class. In that speech, writes Sala-Molins, Condorcet makes "an elegant distinction between the urgency to 'destroy slavery,' [which Condorcet was not demanding], and the time to 'prepare the destruction of slavery,'" which he was (quoted in Sala-Molins 1992a, chapter 3).

The second Enlightenment document to which Sala-Molins pays close scrutiny, in chapter 2 of *Dark Side of the Light,* is the 1789 Declaration of the Rights of Man and of the Citizen. I will present his analysis of its first two articles. The question is normally asked whether the "Man" referred to in the first article of that document ("Men are born and remain free and equal in rights") included such groups as Jews, women, slaves, the non–tax-paying, comedians, actors and so on (Singham 1994, 114–15; Hunt 1996, 16). Making a distinction between a theoretical exclusion and a practical one, an exclusion based on a philosophical premise and one based on the lack of, say, political will, Sala-Molins attempts to show that of the groups mentioned above only the slave was excluded for theoretical reasons, excluded, that is, within the very terms and logic of the document. He arrives at this conclusion in two ways: by focusing on the Preamble to the Declaration, and by reading the Declaration itself, *and insisting that it be read,* side by side with the *Code noir,* which, he reminds the reader, *was still the law of the realm* when the Declaration was proclaimed. In the Preamble it is written:

> The representatives of the French people, constituted as a National Assembly . . . have resolved to set forth in a solemn declaration the natural, inalienable rights of man: so that by

> being constantly present *to all members of the social body,*
> this declaration may always remind them of their rights and
> duties.... (quoted in Sala-Molins 1992a, chapter 2; emphasis
> mine; for the English version, see Hunt 1996, 77)

Now, argues Sala-Molins (1992a, chapter 2), to the extent
that the *Code noir*—the regulating document on slavery—
categorically excluded the slave from the *legal* status of "subject" of the king (the only group to be so excluded on the
grounds of a supposed incomplete humanity or originary
ontological lack),[19] he could not possibly be part of the *social
body* constituted as a National Assembly referred to in the
Declaration. He could not, in other words, be a candidate for
citizenship. Citizenship presupposed subjecthood, the legal
status of subject, which in turn alone authorized membership
of the *social body.* It is precisely this state of legal nonexistence that also makes Article 2—on the "preservation of the
natural and imprescriptible rights of man [to] liberty, property, security and resistance to oppression"—theoretically in-
applicable to the slave. How can he enjoy any rights to property when he is himself "ontologically" and "legally" property,
as *Dark Side of the Light,* pointing to Articles 44–54 of the
Code, puts it (1992a, chapter 2), and how can he enjoy any
right to "resistance to oppression" when all such resistance
is forbidden by law and punishable by death (see Articles 33,
34, 38 of the *Code*)? Clearly then, its later inspirational value
to slaves and other oppressed groups in the French realm and
beyond notwithstanding, the universal subject, "Man" of the
Declaration, referred to just that: the French*man.*

But the exclusion of the slave from citizenship is not limited to Condorcet or the Declaration. Not even Abbé Grégoire
and his Society of the Friends of Blacks seemed to have been
able to avoid this pitfall.[20] In the third and final chapter of his
book, Sala-Molins accuses them of "casuistry" in their attitude to slavery (1992a, chapter 3) and presents them as being

more interested in the suppression of the slave trade and citizenship rights for "people of color" or "mixed race," as they were known then, than in general emancipation. Already in his 1987 book, he highlighted Grégoire's various remarks to the effect that granting citizenship rights to the enslaved blacks in the French Caribbean, as the Convention's 1794 abolition decree had done, was nothing short of "disastrous," the equivalent "in politics of what a volcano is in physics" (Grégoire quoted in Sala-Molins 1987, 263–64). He pointed to the abbot's denial (albeit under a vicious campaign by proslavery deputies who were accusing him of betraying French interests) that he and the Friends ever sought emancipation for blacks. "We are not asking for political rights for the black Frenchmen. . . . No, such an idea has never occurred to us. We said it and wrote it from the founding of our Society" (Grégoire quoted in Sala-Molins 1987, 268). In *Dark Side of the Light,* on the other hand, Sala-Molins focuses on two of the arguments advanced by the Friends for supporting mixed race slaves. The first of these, in spite of its cold cynicism and inadvertent support of slavery, that enfranchised coloreds could be used to control the black slaves and uphold the plantation order (1992a, chapter 3), is only of moderate interest to Sala-Molins. It is the second argument, that being of mixed blood, theirs was a more "accomplished humanity," one more closely French chromatically and therefore culturally and ethically and for that reason deserving of rights, that is of interest to Sala-Molins. He sees this argument as resting on a doctrine of man that was widely shared by Enlightenment thinkers, a doctrine that accounts for the paradox of a theoretically universalistic discourse provincializing itself in practice (to France, at best to Europe) and racializing its scope of application to exclude non-whites. And it is to this paradox and its implications for slavery and, later, colonialism that he devotes most of *Dark Side of Light,* especially the section of chapter 2 titled "Perfectibility and Degeneracy."

Explanations

Of course, as was observed earlier, Sala-Molins is far from being the first to have drawn attention to or analyzed this paradox.[21] Where, perhaps, his approach is different is in the filiation he attempts to establish between the eighteenth-century doctrine of man and medieval, especially Spanish theological, interpretations of the biblical story of the Curse of Ham. This story, it will be recalled, narrates Noah's condemnation in Genesis 9 and 10 of his son Ham (and the latter's descendants, the Canaanites) into the servitude of his brothers Shem and Japheth for having seen him naked. A long tradition of biblical interpretation (coincident with the "massive emergence of Africa in European Letters," Sala-Molins ruefully observes [1987, 22]) "misguidedly" identified Ham and his progeny with "blackness," the peoples of black Africa (Sala-Molins 1992a, chapter 2, n. 29; see also Sollors 1997, 79–111, on the uses and abuses of the Curse of Ham).

Sala-Molins explains the theoretical link made by theologians between the curse and slavery (1987, 20–30). Because the Canaanite (read the inhabitant of sub-Saharan Africa) is a descendant of Noah, he is a human being and therefore cannot be excluded from the possibility of divine grace and salvation. But because of his original curse/sin, he is a lesser human; he is lesser because with the curse comes a loss of the faculties of "rationality," "memory," "intelligence," and "volition," which inhere in the condition of being fully human and are, as Condorcet was later to argue, a sine qua non for the exercise of political sovereignty, of rights. However, not all is lost. Although a lesser human being, the Canaanite can through time, Christian teaching, and conversion to Catholicism (in the eighteenth century both usually provided in slavery) recover his lost faculties and thus his full humanity. The link between this religious interpretation of the curse of Ham and the politics of slavery is clear. It is precisely this doctrine, Sala-Molins argues, that the Enlightenment secularizes.

The medieval religious notions of "perfectibility," of a "fall" from a normative religious ideal of humanity, and of a return to that ideal are all present in the dominant Enlightenment theories of and assumptions about man.[22] What has unmistakably changed, however, is the content of those notions. "Degeneracy" has replaced the notion of a "fall." Varieties of human populations—Laplanders, Amerindians, Asians, blacks from Africa, and so on; non-Europeans in other words—are all seen as exemplifying various degrees of "degeneracy" from the norm, a norm that is white European—in culture, religion, chromatics, and morphology. The accounts for the deviation have also changed. Noah's curse has been replaced by environmental theories of climate, food, and tyrannical government, extensively developed by such thinkers as Montesquieu in Books XIV to XVIII of *The Spirit of Laws,* for example, and the naturalist Buffon (see Cohen 1980, 73–76; Popkin 1973, 250–54; Sloan 1973, 293–322; Sala-Molins 1987, 221–37). "[C]limate," writes Buffon, for example, "is the principal cause of the varieties of mankind. . . . [Air] is necessary to produce the blackness of Negroes. Their children are born white, or rather red, like those of other men. But two or three days after birth their color changes to a yellowish tawny, which grows darker till the seventh or eight day, when they are totally black" (Buffon, *Histoire naturelle* [1748], quoted in Eze 1997, 22–23).[23] It is this belief that "whiteness" is the original color of man that explains the intriguing experiment imagined by Buffon and referred to by Sala-Molins (1992a, chapter 2) to settle a group of blacks in Denmark and proscribe any intermarriage between them and the local Danes to see if their descendants would regain their original "whiteness." Buffon's sincerely held theoretical assumptions convinced him they would.

But whether it is through divine malediction or climate, the result is the same, degeneracy: from a state of spiritual salvation in the case of one, and from human nature or "accomplished humanity" in the other. The solution and its underlying assumptions are also the same. The human being or population that had "deviated"/"degenerated" remains by virtue of the fact of being part of the human species (Enlightenment thinkers were in the main monogenist) "perfectible." In other words she/it can be made to recover her/its lost state of grace in the case of one, or humanity in the other, through Christianization and (French) civilization, respectively.

With this doctrine of man in mind, it is easy to understand why the Enlightenment "stuttered," to borrow Sala-Molins's apt expression, in the face of slavery, why a thinker like Condorcet could not have recommended the immediate emancipation of the slave. The slave needed time (Condorcet's moratorium) to regain the sense of "natural relations" that he had lost as a result of his master's tyranny. One can also better appreciate the priority given by the Friends of Blacks to the emancipation of coloreds. With their part-white heritage, they were much closer than the wholly black slaves to the Enlightenment physical and therefore ethical and cultural ideal of the human. The slippage here, the causal relationship between physique/"race" and culture and ethics, later in the nineteenth century to rigidify into a doctrine of "scientific" racism, is clear. Rights, civilization, and their opposites all became a function of and were determined by skin color and tone and other somatic or phenotypic features. "How moving, this Enlightenment," exclaims Sala-Molins sarcastically (1992a, chapter 2). It proclaims the inalienable rights of all human beings and armed with its anthropological "science," ends up justifying slavery as a redemptive process and laying the intellectual foundations of *the mission civilisatrice* of colonial ideology.

It took the Haitian Revolution of 1791–1804, according to Sala-Molins, to finally put the French Enlightenment in harmony with itself, to make it live up to its promise. In line with the thinking of historian Yves Benot in *La Révolution française et la fin des colonies* (1987) and before him C. L. R. James in *The Black Jacobins* ([1938] 1984), Sala-Molins argues that it is the events of 1791–93 in Haiti and the war with Napoleon of 1802–4 that *imposed* abolition on the Convention and imperial France, respectively. That such a major historical contribution should have gone totally unacknowledged during the 1989 bicentennial celebrations of the French Revolution, during which abolition was presented as an act of charity from a generous and enlightened France, is, according to the Sala-Molins, one of the many shortcomings of those celebrations.

In the epilogue to *Dark Side of the Light,* Sala-Molins imagines the tricentennial of the French Revolution, during which a France possessed of a true sense of universal justice and by then secure in its identity as a multiethnic society finally acknowledges the contribution of black Haiti, and as it rightly did Monge, Condorcet and Grégoire in 1989, receives into the Pantheon one of its greatest revolutionary leaders, the former slave and black Frenchman Toussaint Louverture.

Demurrings

Dark Side of the Light does not leave the reader indifferent, and it is conceivably open to various objections, especially from the specialist reader. I would like to conclude this introduction by raising some of the more general critical points that could be made against the book. The first is that the book engages in a retrospective trial and uses a late-twentieth-century sensibility on the issues of race and slavery and knowledge accumulated since the eighteenth century to judge eighteenth-century positions on them. Although seemingly valid, this objection is not applicable to this book, because French Enlightenment thinkers were not themselves moral relativists. So when Sala-Molins insists that ethical perspectives should not be situational, he is doing no more than holding those thinkers to their moral universalism.

Slavery, he wrote, "should not be trivialized by invoking, as is always done, the question of the gap between today's moral demands and the easy-going attitude of the people of that period" (1992a, chapter 2). Two hundred years before the Enlightenment, he reminds the reader, there were already individuals like the Andalusian theologian Bartolomé Las Casas, who unambiguously rejected the various interpretations by Spanish neoscholastics to justify the enslavement of Amerindians and later of Africans using Aristotle's theory of natural slavery (1992a, 57; 1987, 43–48), and who, with other Spanish theologians, even managed to convince Charles V to outlaw the enslavement of Amerindians in 1530. And long before them, he observes, was Saint Augustine, who, asked what he thought of the extraordinary ancient Greek tales about antipodean humans, headless and with faces stuck in their chests, replied simply:

> Rubbish in all likelihood. I ask to see, but fear there is nothing to see. But if they truly exist, why should that bother me? Their shape and color matter not. They think; they are therefore human beings like you and me, because in them, reason is the image of God. (Saint Augustine, quoted in Sala-Molins, 1992a, 59)

Finally, Sala-Molins gives the example of the Spanish monk Peter Claver (1581–1654), who spent his life taking care of sick and dying slaves (1992a, 56). In the *Code noir* (3), he even gives the example of the American Quakers, who only armed with their faith and no noisy philosophical theory of rights fought relentlessly for abolition.

If Sala-Molins makes many positive references to Christian theologians in a book on the Enlightenment, it is partly to deflate the superior anti–Christian religion pretensions of the latter. Sala-Molins devotes several deliciously ironic and philosophically dense passages in chapter 2 of his book to the paradox of a religion dismissed as a farrago of "prejudice" and "superstition" by the Enlightenment and yet turning out to be a surer guide to ethical choices in the area of slavery than all the enlightened "science" of the Enlighteners. In a position similar to that of *Dialectic of the Enlightenment* (1–34), Sala-Molins seems to suggest that one of the pitfalls of the Enlightenment lay in its attempt to establish and rely on totally scientific-rationalist grounds for ethical judgments and meaning, to abjure myth, religion, and the nonrational, to dismiss them as error and superstition. While such grounds are indeed essential and are a bulwark against intolerance and fanaticism—not to talk of the liberating understanding and control of the natural world to which they have led—their tight conflation with the ethical, the belief that they provide the surest and only groundwork for morals, can also lead to moral disasters.

Sala-Molins's use of the word *genocide* (in the December 9, 1948, United Nations definition of that term; see Sala-Molins 1987, 18) to describe the half-millennium-long Atlantic trade in slaves, and the parallel he establishes in his preface to *Dark Side of the Light* between this event and the Holocaust, even slightly reformulating Adorno's famous dictum—about writing poetry after Auschwitz (Adorno 1967, 34) into "How is thinking possible after Saint-Domingue?" (1992a, preface)—suggest the influence of or at least an engagement with Horkheimer and Adorno's much debated thesis of a link between the Enlightenment and the Holocaust (Sutcliffe 2003; Schechter 2001).[24] It certainly suggests a view—similar to Horkheimer and Adorno's on the Holocaust—of Atlantic slavery as absolute evil, radical unrepresentability. While Sala-Molins is too much of a product of the Enlightenment to exclusively ground truth and knowledge, including moral truth, in intuition and revelation, he is nonetheless skeptical of traditions of thought that make no room for what he calls "mystery." "If the Enlightenment failed," he writes, "it is precisely because it sacrificed the mystery of the human, as it was called in the past, to a concern with scientific transparency" (1992a, chapter 2).

A second objection that could be made against *Dark Side of the Light* is that eschewing its own method of approaching slavery "from the bottom," it reduces the French Enlightenment's attitudes to slavery to only the texts of elite thinkers. Historian Marie Shanti Singham points to the existence of non-elite, antislavery patriotic writings in France that were unambiguous in their opposition to Caribbean slavery, which they saw as the tropical expression of a similar fate for the dispossessed poor and working-class whites in France (Singham 1994, 136–38). In other words, the dichotomy should not be between an uncompromising Christian doctrine on the one hand and an ambivalent Enlightenment thought on the other. Just as there were Christian theologians who justified the practice of slavery, and against whom Las Casas did battle, so there were principled Enlightenment abolitionists. To which I suppose Sala-Molins would reply that since the latter made no exaggerated claims, avoided being self-righteous, and have not been celebrated in France, they do not open themselves to criticism.

A third objection that could be formulated against *Dark Side of the Light* is that of insensitivity to the historical context (French rivalry with England and Spain, powerful proslavery interests) in which men like Condorcet and Grégoire were operating, a context that therefore demanded, indeed, imposed compromise, if even the smallest gains were to be registered. Grégoire's denial in the National Assembly, referred to above, about ever having thought of emancipating black slaves was made literally to protect himself from campaigns of treason that had been launched against him and the Friends. Condorcet, in his speech on planters also referred to above, pointed to "injustices that cannot be repaired in a day, and which, tied to political interests . . . can only be destroyed with the care necessary to ensure the good" (quoted in Sala-Molins 1992a, chapter 3). Sala-Molins's reply to this would of course be that while real, what such a context conceals are the personal economic stakes in slavery of some of the Enlighteners themselves, and he points, for example, to Montesquieu's investment in slave shipping companies.

The 1989 Bicentennial Celebrations Re-visioned

But whether the interests are national or personal is ultimately of little significance. What is of cardinal importance to Sala-Molins is the conviction that commercial interests should never have the better of principled opposition to injustice. This conviction animates with a passion the entire book and provides the link between its immediate concern, the Enlightenment, and France in the 1980s and early 1990s—the socialist France of President François Mitterrand, the France of the bicentennial celebration of the Revolution. If socialist France celebrated French Enlightenment thought and the Revolution with such excess, reducing it all to spectacle, according to Sala-Molins, it is because it recognized itself in that thought (1992a, chapter 3). Both the Enlightenment and socialist France were high on grandiloquence but short on results. Both abandoned their ethical projects: slave emancipation in the case of one and social justice in the other. For socialist France, he gives as examples of such abandonment the violent repression of the demands for sovereignty from France in 1984 of the Kanak people of New Caledonia, the (then) new immigration and restrictive citizenship laws voted by the National Assembly, the sale by France the world over of military hardware as if it were "melons," the deregulation (very relative in the case of France) of the economy, thus leaving the economically weak at the mercy of those he calls the "sharks," and so on (1992a, chapter 3). Both also justified that abandonment in terms of the need for "realism," "national commercial interests," and "consensuality." In socialist France, writes Sala-Molins, the government promotes

> [the] holy virtue of consensus (this kind of thing that
> could be described as the secularization of a "holy commu-
> nion"). . . . we retain in our references to the Enlightenment,
> the Revolution, and their aftermath, the words and actions
> that made for good relations even if that meant disaster.
> (1992a, chapter 3)

To readers familiar with the Franco-French quarrels sur-rounding the bicentennial celebrations, it is clear that the reference to "consensus" here is to that event. To avoid what Steven Kaplan in his book on those celebrations calls "ruin-ous debate" (1995, 21), the government of President Mitterrand sought national consensus—the word became a by-word for the organizers—(see Kaplan 1995, 25–37) on an "essential core" of values that could be celebrated (Kaplan 1995, 26). This core—freedom, democracy, and human *(political)* rights—still left many people dissatisfied, and one such expression of dis-satisfaction from the French Radical, and possibly Marxist, Left is *Dark Side of the Light.* To Sala-Molins, the choice of and emphasis on *political* over *social* rights by Mitterrand's government, its "droit-de-l'hommisme" (rights-of-manism) as it was unsympathetically termed (Kaplan 1995, 35), were not ideologically innocent. It was the expression of social-ist France's abdication to what Kaplan calls the neoliberal emphasis of the New Global World Order, an order, as Sala-Molins sees it, that privileges freedom over economic and so-cial justice. In short, to him Mitterrand had evacuated "revo-lution from the Revolution" (1992a, chapter 3). He had served up a bourgeois, liberal version of the latter. To proponents of the government's democracy and *"political* rights" position, on the other hand, these values are defended as indispensable to growth and social development. These are complex debates, to an extent typically French, and fascinatingly discussed by

Kaplan. To the extent that *Dark Side of the Light* is an intervention in them, even if on the mode of polemics, allusiveness, and derision, it is as much a work of cultural criticism of eighteenth-century French Enlightenment attitudes to slavery as it is of late-twentieth-century socialist France and its reading of the Enlightenment.

In the course of translating *Les Misères des Lumières: Sous la raison, l'outrage,* I have enjoyed the goodwill, and benefited from the help, of a number of people. I am grateful to Professor Louis Sala-Molins for his helpful replies to my queries as I worked on the translation. My special thanks go to Professor Karlis Racevskis, my colleague at Ohio State University, for bringing the book to my attention and for his warm, collegial encouragement after I decided to translate it. He made many invaluable comments and suggestions for improvement on my translation manuscript for which I am grateful.

I wish to acknowledge the reviewers of my translation project proposal, two of them anonymous, for their comments on Sala-Molins's book. Although these comments were made long before I conceived the introduction to the book, they contributed to aspects of my thinking about the book when I eventually came to write the introduction. I also thank my friend Professor C. Sholé Johnson of Middle State Tennessee University for his useful suggestions, and Professor Pius Ngandu Nkashama of Louisiana State University for our long-distance, sometimes odd-hour, discussions on the book.

Finally, my thanks go to Richard Morrison, acquisitions editor at the University of Minnesota Press, for his support for and confidence in this project.

Notes

This title of this introduction is a variation on Robin May Schott's fine article "The Gender of the Enlightenment" (1996, 471–81).

1. For an account of these events, see Levine (1961).

2. See Jean-Pierre Vittori (2001) and Paul Aussaresses (2001).

3. For the full provisions of the law, see the *Journal Officiel de la République française,* 119 (May 23, 2001): 8175.

4. Translation mine; all translations are mine unless otherwise indicated.

5. The complete text of his speech, "Esclavage: Le droit à réparations," is available in the newspaper *L'Humanité* of March 12, 2000. Sala-Molins was very critical in his speech of the Lower House of the French National Assembly for emasculating the original bill, which had included provisions for moral, legal, and material responsibility and reparations for France. In the end only moral responsibility was retained, which is why he enjoined the Senate, unsuccessfully, to reject the bill. For his discussion of the issue of types of responsibility and the need for France to accept all three and make good on them, see Sala-Molins (1987, x-xiv).

6. Rousseau writes: "The right of slavery is null, not only because it is illegitimate, but also because it is absurd. These words *slavery* and *right* are contradictory. The one excludes the other" (quoted in Sala-Molins 1987, 238; trans. F. Watkins, Rousseau, *Political Writings* [London: Nelson], 12).

7. The relevant *Code noir* article reads, "Déclarons les esclaves être meubles, et comme tels entrer dans la communauté . . ." [Let us declare that slaves are chattel, and that they enter into the community as such . . ." (178)].

8. Throughout this article in references to slaves, I will be using interchangeably and in a dis-engendered sense feminine adjectives and pronouns and the masculine equivalents.

9. For a study of the image of the Enlightenment and the Revolution during the bicentennial celebrations of the French Revolution, see Kaplan (1995).

10. For some contemporary French reactions to *Le Code noir,* see Sala-Molins (1987, vii-xvi, 1–6).

11. Sala-Molins acknowledges the work of such pioneers as Duchet (1971) and pays special tribute to W. B. Cohen, on whose 1980 book, *The French Encounter with Africans,* he generously draws. For examples of earlier and also more recent studies of the theme of Enlightenment and race, see Curtin (1964, 3–57, 227–44); Popkin

(1973, 245–62); Sloan (1973, 293–322); Biondi (1985, 191–97); Gilroy (1993, 1–40); Singham (1994, 114–53); Eze (1997); Williams (1998, 67–80); and Johnson (2003, 147–74).

12. This book might seem less unconventional to an educated English-language readership than it would be to its French-reading counterpart. Perhaps because of the national distance from the phenomenon and the possibility of detachment that this brings, a critical engagement with the Enlightenment and race seems to have been present much longer in the writings of English-language literary critics, intellectuals, and cultural historians. See note 11 above.

13. For a classic application of the practice of reading the literature and cultural production of the metropole from the latter's margins, internal as well as external, see Bhabha (1990, especially 1–7, 197–212, 231–49, 291–322).

14. For a forceful discussion of the need for universalist principles in the struggle against injustice, see Bronner (1995, 1–17). Bronner illustrates this need with the example of Nelson Mandela, who, he writes, "of course knew better" [than to reject these universal principles]. Bronner continues: "The fact of the matter is that the most successful and emancipatory movements of the oppressed were all inspired by a commitment to either a language of rights or universalist principles" (13). Also see Eagleton (2003, 103–39). For the tension between the need for such principles and their limitations in the context of feminist politics, see Flax (1993, 67–89).

15. See, for example, Williams (1999, 308–16). The only sections he excerpts from *Réflexions* relate to Condorcet's critique of slavery but not to Condorcet's objections to the immediate emancipation of the slaves.

16. On Las Casas's notion of sovereignty and its rearticulation by Enlightenment thinkers, see Sala-Molins (1987, 25–30, especially note 7).

17. For a discussion of Condorcet on slavery, see Williams (1998, 67–80).

18. For a succinct and helpful analysis of this philosophical distinction, see Johnson (2003, 153–54).

19. Other groups like Jews, women, comedians, the propertyless, and so on were excluded from rights, Sala-Molins contends, for religious, professional, social, or economic reasons, but not, as in the

case of the black slaves, because of a supposed originary lack, one cosubstantial with "blackness," which made it impossible for them to belong to the French *social body.* Those groups, he wrote, "were neither dispossessed of their humanity, nor of their membership of the social body, because no one dared banish them from the . . . community of subjects" to that of incomplete humans—in an ethico-cultural sense, and for some thinkers, in a physical one (1992a, chapter 2). This, of course, is why they were not and could not be reduced to the status of pure objects of monetary value, be enslaved in other words. For details on the notion of an originary lack, see Sala-Molins (1987, 74–79; 1992a, 38–41) and the section of this introduction titled "Explanations." For the classification in the eighteenth century of varieties of human populations along the lines of a Great Chain of Being, see Sala-Molins (1987, 25–35) and Cohen (1980, 86–94).

20. On the Society of the Friends of Blacks in antislavery thought and politics, see Necheles (1973, 355–68), Sala-Molins (1987, 261–74), Dorigny (2000), and Singham (1994, 131–39).

21. See note 11 above.

22. For other eighteenth-century theories of man—pre-Adamism and polygenism, for example—see Popkin (1973, 250–54) and Cohen (1980, 84–86).

23. For a useful collection of eighteenth- and nineteenth-century writings on race, see Eze (1997).

24. Sala-Molins, it must be emphasized, does not establish a causal relationship between the Enlightenment and slavery. To do so would obviously be foolish given that the Atlantic slave trade and Caribbean slavery were practiced long before the Enlightenment. What he does, however, is show how the latter gave comfort to French slavers by providing them with a philosophical justification for it.

Works Cited

Adorno, Theodor. 1967. "Cultural Criticism and Society." In *Prisms,* trans. Samuel and Sherry Weber, 19–34. London: Neville Spearman.

Aussaresses, Paul. 2001. *Services spéciaux: Mon témoignage sur la torture.* Paris: Perrin.

Benot, Yves, *La Revolution française et la fin des colonies.* Paris: Editions La Découverte, [1987] 2004.

Bhabha, Homi, ed. 1990. *Nation and Narration.* London: Routledge.

Biondi, Carmenella. 1985. "L'Afrique des philosophes: Lien mythique, terre d'hommes ou entrepôt de marchandises?" In *L'Homme des Lumières et la découverte de l'autre,* ed. D. Droixhe and Pol-P. Gossiaux, 191–97. Bruxelles: L'Université de Bruxelles.

Bronner, Stephen. 1995. "The Great Divide: The Enlightenment and its Critics." *New Politics* 5, 3 (Summer): 1–17.

Cohen, W. B. 1980. *The French Encounter with Africans: White Response to Blacks, 1530–1880.* Bloomington: Indiana University Press.

Condorcet (J. A. N. de Caritat). 1788. *Réflexions sur l'esclavage de nègres.* (Written under the pseudonym, M. Schwartz). Neufchâtel: Société Typographique.

Curtin, Philip. 1964. *The Image of Africa: British Ideas and Action.* Madison: University of Wisconsin Press.

Darnton, George. 1997. "George Washington's False Teeth," *New York Review of Books,* March 27, 34–38.

Derrida, Jacques. 1999. *Sur parole: Instantanés philosophiques.* Paris: Editions de l'Aube.

Dorigny, Marcel. 2000. "Grégoire et le combat contre l'esclavage pendant la Révolution." In *Grégoire et la cause des noirs 1789–1831,* ed. Yves Benot and Marcel Dorigny. Saint-Denis: Société française d'histoire d'outre-mer.

Duchet, Michel. 1971. *Anthropologie et histoire au siècle des Lumières.* Paris: Albin Michel.

Eagleton, Terry. 2003. *After Theory.* New York: Basic Books.

Eze, Emmanuel. 1997. *Race and the Enlightenment: A Reader.* Oxford: Blackwell Publishers.

Flax, Jane. 1993. "Postmodernism and Gender Relations in Feminist Theory." In *Revising the Word and the World: Essays in Feminist Literary Criticism,* ed. Vévé A. Clark, Ruth-Ellen B. Joeres, and Madelon Sprengnether. Chicago: University of Chicago Press.

Ghachem, Malick. 2000. "Montesquieu in the Caribbean: The Colonial Enlightenment between *Code noir* and *Code civil.*" In *Postmodernism and the French Enlightenment: New Perspectives in Eighteenth-Century French Intellectual History,* ed. Daniel Gordon, 1–30. New York: Routledge.

Gilroy, Paul. 1993. *The Black Atlantic: Modernity and Double Consciousness.* Boston: Harvard University Press.

Horkheimer, Max, and Theodor Adorno. [1947] 2002. *Dialectic of Enlightenment.* Trans. Edmund Jephcott. Stanford, CA: Stanford University Press.

Hunt, Lynn. 1996. *The French Revolution and Human Rights.* Boston: St. Martin's Press.

James, C. L. R. [1938] 1984. *The Black Jacobins.* London: Allison and Busby.

Jelen, Brigitte. 2002. "17 Octobre 1961–17 Octobre 2001: Une commémoration ambiguë." *French Politics, Culture, and Society* 20, 1.

Johnson, Clarence Sholé. 2003. *Cornel West and Philosophy: The Quest for Social Justice.* New York: Routledge.

Journal Officiel de la République française, 119 May, 2001.

Kaplan, Steven, L. 1995. *Farewell Revolution: Disputed Legacies, France 1789/1989.* Ithaca, NY: Cornell University Press.

Levine, Michel. 1961. *Les ratonnades d'octobre: Un meurtre collectif.* Paris: Seuil.

Necheles, Ruth. 1973. "Grégoire and the Egalitarian Movement." In *Racism in the Eighteenth Century,* ed. Harold Pagliaro. Cleveland: Case Western Reserve University.

Paxton, Robert. 1972. *Vichy France: Old Guard and New Order 1940–1944.* New York: Knopf.

Popkin, Richard. 1973. "The Philosophical Basis of Eighteenth Century Racism." In *Racism in the Eighteenth Century,* ed. Harold Pagliaro. Cleveland: Case Western Reserve University.

Racevskis, Karlis. 1998. *Modernity's Pretenses: Making Reality Fit Reason from "Candide" to the Gulag.* New York: State University at New York Press.

Sala-Molins, Louis. [1987] 2003. *Le Code noir ou le calvaire de Canaan.* Paris: PUF.

———. 1992a. *Les Misères des Lumières: Sous la raison, l'outrage.* Paris: Laffont.

———. 1992b. *L'Afrique aux Amériques: Le Code Noir espagnol.* Paris: PUF.

———. 1999. "Esclavage: Une mémoire à peu de frais." *Le Monde,* February 23, 15.

———. 2000. "Esclavage: Le droit à réparations." *L'Humanité,* March 12. (www.humanité.presse.fr/journal/2000-03-21/2000-03-21-222092).

———. 2002a. "L'esclavage, un tabou français." *Historia Thématique,* no. 080.

———. 20002b. "Le Code noir est le texte juridique le plus monstrueux de l'histoire moderne." *Historia Thématique,* no. 080.

Schechter, Ronald. 2001. "Rationalizing the Enlightenment: Post-modernism and Theories of Anti-Semitism," in *Postmodernism and the Enlightenment: New Perspectives in Eighteenth-Century French Intellectual History,* ed. Daniel Gordon, 93–116. New York and London: Routledge.

Schott, Robin May. 1996. "The Gender of the Enlightenment." In *What Is Enlightenment: Eighteenth-Century Answers and Twentieth-Century Questions,* ed. James Schmidt. Berkeley: University of California Press.

Singham, Marie Shanti. 1994. "Betwixt Cattle and Men: Jews, Blacks, and Women, and the Declaration of Human Rights." In *The French Idea of Freedom: The Old Regime and the Declaration of Rights of 1789,* ed. Dale Van Kley. Stanford, CA: Stanford University Press.

Sloan, Philip. 1973. "The Idea of Racial Degeneracy in Buffon's *Histoire naturelle.*" In *Racism in the Eighteenth Century,* ed. Harold Pagliaro, 293–322. Cleveland: Case Western Reserve University.

Sollors, Werner. 1997. *Neither Black nor White: Thematic Explorations in Interracial Literature.* Oxford: Oxford University Press.

Sutcliffe, Adam. 2003. *Judaism and Enlightenment.* Cambridge: Cambridge University Press.

Vittori, Jean-Pierre Vittori. 2001. *On a torturé en Algérie.* Paris: Ramsey.

Williams, David. 1998. "Condorcet and the Politics of Black Servitude." In *Making Connections,* ed. J. Dolamore. Bern and New York: Peter Lang.

———, ed. 1999. *The Enlightenment.* London: Cambridge University Press.

Dark Side
of the Light

SLAVERY AND THE FRENCH ENLIGHTENMENT

Preface

Imperial France condemned Toussaint Louverture to die of cold and hunger in the Jura. Republican and socialist France provided Duvalier with an imperial retirement. How do you, a Haitian, react to this paradox?

It was December 1989, a week before the transfer to the Pantheon of the remains of Monge, Condorcet, and Abbé Grégoire. I was on my way to the Caribbean to attend a colloquium on the meaning of the French Revolution in that region at the time, notably in Haiti. Next to me, during one leg of the journey, was a Haitian journalist. Was it coincidence or providence? The answer depends on the Enlightenment, which did not believe in providence, or on "prejudice," "this science" of theologians that lives by it and blesses it. So it was coincidence. The Haitian journalist and I talk about one thing and another. I am burning to ask him the question. What's the sense of resisting? I go ahead and ask it. His reply is immediate: "Where then is the paradox? France has always done us so much harm." I was not expecting such a reply. My

3

mind's ear was all cocked to enjoy a good argument, probably critical, even ferocious, but not such a peremptory and lapidary reply.

The Haitian journalist had struck me as thoughtful in our conversation up to that point. He remained so even after we had drifted to other subjects. Am I right to conclude from this that it was quite simply his way of reacting to my somewhat tasteless reference in the same breath to Toussaint the giant and Duvalier the bandit? My fellow passenger lost no time in softening his reply by invoking various grounds deriving from the imperatives of history to explain the scandal of the imprisonment and death of Toussaint, or aspects of international law to justify the scandal of Duvalier's gilded exile. And it did not occur to me, not even remotely, to suggest to him, even with a hesitant "come on," that this was mere whitewashing. Such a suggestion, to my mind, would have seemed rude, indecent, and obscene. The Haitian, for me, was a dramatic reminder of the existence of a right that, like some other rights, defines the humanity of man: the right to memory, even, and especially when the essence of such a right takes the form of resentment or revolt.

But my short-term neighbor was "all over black, and with such a flat nose" that I ought to have felt "mercy" and "pity" for him.[1] Should I not have taken into account, out of mercy and pity, his inability to observe a distance between himself and his history, between his people and their history, and used the opportunity to enlighten him a bit and usher him gently unto the threshold of a less intemperate judgment?

This is what is generally done. Arguments are laid out, issues are weighed, analyzed, and "put in perspective." Passions are cooled down. In short, the black man is taught, taught to cast on his history by whatever style deemed appropriate— bullying, mockery, encouragement—the dispassionate look that it deserves: that of the white man. He is begged not to let himself be carried away by hasty generalizations born of passion, but which, thank goodness, can be set straight by reason. Blacks enjoy that: learning from whites the art of dispassionate and rigorous judgment, the consummate one of making History carry the weight of their histories. Blacks, we had suspected all along, but are now confirmed in our belief by Hegel and Hugo,[2] have no history. How then can they exhibit the consciousness of a history they have not had? No one died of hunger and cold in Fort-de-Joux. No one lives in gilded retirement under our gentle skies, as we said in our conversation.

When you have no history, could you, from the ocean of bestiality, have truly beached one day on the shores of humanity? It is difficult to imagine this, even more to affirm it. But what if blacks still run up against a denial of their humanity even among those who would be extremely irritated to be thought of as harboring the slightest racist tendencies? Their right to memory, if they have it, is not acknowledged. They are constantly reminded that the right to resentment, if they think they have it, they stole, but that it was not granted them. As for their right to revolt, we would like to impose a time frame for its exercise.

To pose the issue of the poverty of the Enlightenment right away, let us consider the example of the most cold-hearted form of genocide by Modernity: that which accompanied Modernity from its dawn, remained with it throughout its course and well beyond it, getting bogged down in nothingness only in the twilight years of the nineteenth century and well into the contemporary period; a form of genocide that did not take place on the sly but in full view of everyone; one whose efficiency did not derive from the madness of bandits or from coded messages decipherable only by initiates but from very Christian members of royalty, solemn decrees and privileges, and from a legal code drawn up in clear language, publicized everywhere and readable by all; a form of genocide that did not cross out from humanity—on the basis of some assessment of degeneracy—the offspring of such and such a stateless people, of humans guilty of abnormal sexual practices, but one that banished from humanity an entire continent, on the basis of a body deemed bestial and a mind considered fit for natural enslavement.

Who, except in a moment of unbridled and corrupt revisionism, will have the effrontery to ask a Jew, a Gypsy, a homosexual (the homosexual, it is true, will be asked to keep quiet, always out of decency or respect for the memory of Jews, rarely of Gypsies) to forego his resentment, to forget? Who will ask them to control their passion and talk of their situation only with the restraint befitting reason? No one.

Who will question the capacity of Jews to keep a cool head, whatever their emotions, knowing full well that describing the "final solution" with all the words expressive of its monstrosity, grotesque excesses, and absolute horror is already to keep a cool head? No one. An expression in the form of a question that would become famous is:

How is thinking possible after Auschwitz?

And yet people have continued to think. They have thought Auschwitz even at the risk of rambling off into madness by getting too close to the gas chambers.

Human beings have done all that to fellow humans. Whites have done it to other whites. The Christian district of the European continent did that to the Jews who had been living there for centuries. Whites, through other whites, sent their fellow whites—a certain "species" of white (to reason for a moment like evildoers) whose only crime was to exist—to their death. This tragedy lasted a good many years, and everyone swore never to forget it.

Elsewhere, for centuries, whites from the Christian district of Europe, through other whites and blacks, eradicated from the ranks of humanity as many of the latter as they could because of their color. Whites decreed once and for all—with repercussions that were felt for centuries—that all blacks could be raided and enslaved because, in truth, they were already slaves. Who will have the effrontery to ask blacks to forget their resentment, to forget, to control their passion and to talk about their situation with the restraint befitting reason? A legion.

Who will question the ability of blacks to keep a cool head, whatever their emotions, knowing full well that qualifying the slave trade and slavery with all the words expressive of their monstrosity, grotesque excesses, and absolute horror is already to keep a cool head? Everyone.

Who has ever asked the question: "How is thinking possible after Saint Domingue?" People have quietly continued to think after Saint-Domingue with no qualms. Indeed, thinking on Saint-Domingue has continued. The cleverest concepts are worked out at two paces, two phrases from the sugar-cane mills, in the death alleys of slaves. Has so much thinking, and in such peremptory terms, ever been done as during the *Aufklärung,* the Enlightenment?

Can the black man demand, if not for that period then at least for today, that the so-called universal significance of a thinking that chooses to ignore him—and that in so doing dislodges him from the category of the human—be appraised in light of the centuries-old, transcontinental disaster of the slave trade and slavery? No, he has no right to do that. What if he does it all the same? He is then accused of being mad. Let him reread Hegel and Hugo, and if he has the least bit of sense, he will understand the absurdity of his impatience. In short, the black man is not credible when he speaks about himself. But, of course, when we speak about him or ourselves, we are, or can be. When he speaks about us, he is accused of meddling in what does not concern him, namely his history. Should he talk to us about himself, we conclude that he is engaged in a monologue of his wounded subjectivity, and *that* is of no interest to us.

I might as well now state, without spending an eternity on preambles, what I propose to remind the reader about. It is depressingly banal.

The Enlightenment composes the music, fills it with the most beautiful harmonies of a grand symphony to the glory of Reason, Man, the Sovereignty of the individual, and universal Philanthropy. This score is being beautifully performed until suddenly a black man erupts in the middle of the concert. What at that point becomes of Man, Sovereignty, Reason, Philanthropy? They disappear into thin air. And the beautiful music pierces your eardrums with the gratings of sarcasm.

Clearly, the crucial test case for the Enlightenment is the slave trade and slavery. It is not the Jew, as it is sometimes claimed, or Woman, as it is often stated. It is the "slave." For those who read and reread the score today, in this age of enthusiastic return to the Enlightenment because of an alleged definitive failure of all else, the crucial test still concerns the "Negro" slaves.

To interpret the Enlightenment without them is to play the game of the Enlightenment: it is tantamount to limiting universal philanthropy to one's little neighborhood, reason to the domain of "biblico-whitism," sovereignty to the boundaries of the parish, and the accomplished individual to the achievements of our local landowner. And, goodness gracious, the fact that this horizontal flattening of the vertical hierarchies of distribution would muddle and murder some good things in the Old Regime is hardly insignificant. But that is not all, far from it.

Now, it is being claimed repeatedly and emphasized ad nauseam that this is the major achievement of the Enlightenment. But right in the middle of this chorus the slave knows, from a body furrowed by the whip and pierced by nails, torn at the stake, contaminated by the rapist slaver, that nothing really was achieved.

Oh, the majestic grandeur of fire, which in Saint-Domingue

pitted against the Enlightenment the major and minor premises and the conclusion of one of the most beautiful syllogisms that History—spelt with as many upper-case letters as one would care to waste on the word—ever succeeded in formulating in an outburst of fire!

Let us restrict our discussion of the Enlightenment to within the latter's time frame so that no one may use arguments from Montaigne, La Boétie, or Rabelais to save the honor of a school of thought whose omissions and blind spots are as significant as its breathtaking insights and dazzling recklessness. Let us start then from where it all started: with Montesquieu and not earlier. And let us conclude, necessarily, at the point when it all came to an end: with Napoleon's vast military expedition to Saint-Domingue, with Monsieur de Noailles's dogs, and not later.

During this entire period, slavery constituted an inescapable reality whose gigantic economic importance, cultural stakes, and political and judicial aberration could not, without bad faith or mental blindness, be ignored.

How can the Enlightenment be interpreted? Only with the *Code noir* in hand.[3] In a partisan way? No, in an intellectually honest one. Is the Spanish Golden Century not interpreted against the background glow of the stakes of the papal inquisition? What nocturnal iridescences are commonly used to interpret German romanticism? My aim here is to read the Enlightenment from the position of the slaves, from the side of darkness, a darkness that the Enlightenment did not create but that it did not dissipate either because it did not throw light on it. Only to speak of black slaves? I propose to make my way from absolute nonsense to the sensible rigor of the best arguments and to test these against the fact of slavery. We will then see which arguments will stand and which will collapse. We will then know whether it is appropriate or not to endorse Herder's description of the men of the Enlightenment as "the flatterers of their century."[4]

While examining the views of the Enlightenment, it will also be useful to see what some of today's complacently self-styled and so-called philosophers or thinkers have had to say about the Enlightenment. We shall take note of their silences. It will then be tempting to conclude that like the eighteenth century, ours is not lacking in flatterers.

CHAPTER 1

Condorcet, "Lamenting"

For any serious study of anthropology in the age of the Enlightenment, the work of Michèle Duchet is compulsory reading.[1] Meticulous in its analyses and balanced in its conclusions, this work paints a rather unflattering picture of the way in which French Enlightenment thought mapped out the symbolic geography of the human and the inhuman. With admirable clarity and unrelenting vigor, it shows that all the French thinkers of the age—the major as well as the minor ones, Raynal and Diderot included—failed to interrogate colonial conquest and domination, that they cast their arguments within a framework that King and Navy found not only acceptable but was actively promoted as a way of counterbalancing, from the top, the arrogant excesses of the colonists. Raynal was a court favorite, while Diderot enjoyed a pension from a shipping company involved in trade—who knows what kind?—between Africa, the Caribbean, and France.

From the research that has been carried out on our great thinkers, one fact stands out with clarity, namely, that there was no question of considering the black population, freed or enslaved, of the Caribbean and the other colonies (assuming the word *population* is appropriate), as constituting peoples, let alone nations. It was in the interests and within the rights of metropolitan France to derive maximum benefits from the colonies. More profits could probably, almost certainly, be made if the people who cultivated the land there could catch a glimpse of a hopeful future beyond their present disastrous condition.

It was considered just and moral to enrich oneself in the colonies. But the slave trade desperately lacked an aesthetic dimension. The triangular shipping business was not only charming as a consequence of the real problems of "packaging" and "management" of the cargo, it raised a number of philosophical issues. In the long run, Justice and Goodness (and for that matter Beauty and Truth too) demanded that the inevitable be accepted, that the Negro slave—movable assets of his master[2]—be changed to a black worker, a subject, or almost one, of His Very Catholic Majesty. It is well known that the fits of impatience of the *philosophes* adorned with wigs and lace concerned at most only the situation of mulattoes, of people of mixed blood, whose blackness could legally, with no harmful effects, be whitened by a spot of European blood. For the blacks—whose biological being had not been regenerated by the slightest touch of Europeanness—it was thought normal, moral, logical, and politic to wait.

To wait for what? For the creation of the legal and procreative conditions for the gradual whitening, and the development of the appropriate context for philosophical receptiveness to white virtue. To a virtue that would not necessarily be Catholic or canonical but certainly European and rational. Such then, concerning blacks, is the truth of the universal philanthropy of the Enlightenment, the truth that shines through our philosophy and history textbooks; such is the conclusion that Michèle Duchet courageously and dispassionately draws at the end of her analyses.

Among the very best of the *philosophes,* the emphasis was on the "feasibility" of making a subject out of the slave, a human being out of the Negro through the adoption of two different approaches: different and yet—in the mind of their proponents and in terms of the results they expected—convergent. The slave trade had to be abolished, and a schedule of emancipation established. It goes without saying that between the drying up of the market as a result of the desired abolition and the end of the moratorium—in other words, between the elevation of the slave from "movable asset" to "subject"—the cultivation of the sugarcane, indigo, cotton, and tobacco fields had to continue, the mills had to keep grinding; in short, the inescapable economic imperatives of metropolitan France had to remain unquestioned.

It thus became necessary to work out a "royal path" from slavery to emancipation. One that was slow, clear in its layout, and protected from start to finish. The black man would no longer be hunted in Africa; he would be bred and raised on the spot.

At Thirty-five, You Will Become a Human Being, My Son

On this issue, the imagination of writers remained ever fertile. Their thinking clearly shows that the very best were incapable—a point I will return to later in the section on the young Negro child in a boudoir—of treating the black man as a human being, as anything other than an indispensable element in the efficient running of the economic and domestic system:

> We propose therefore not to free Negroes the moment they are born, but to grant their masters the right to raise and use them as slaves on condition they are freed at the age of thirty-five.

As was decreed by the *Code noir,* slaves could not marry without the consent of their masters. "Pregnant Negresses" were to be closely watched to prevent their masters from working them to exhaustion or from treating them harshly with the sole aim of making them abort. They would receive monthly visits from a specialist; a precise accounting of the number of pregnancies, abortions, and births would be kept. These laws on phased emancipation were obviously to come into effect on a specific day. From the judicious mix of the effects of these and other legal provisions, let me quote, for the enlightenment of the reader, a few choice examples: "Negroes under fifteen at the time this law is published will be declared free at the age of forty." Those above fifteen on that memorable date shall remain in chains until they are fifty; then they shall be asked to choose "either to remain with their masters, or to enter a public institution where they will be fed." Births would be facilitated and the number of emancipations increased.

The text in question goes on to state with the most touching serenity the double, and unquestionable, imperative of maintaining production on the one hand and, on the other, of ensuring the progress of the Negro in the rediscovery of his human nature (of which he has lost all notion) and of free labor:

> This piece of legislation would have none of the disadvantages normally feared from sudden changes, since emancipation would only be done in stages. The law would give time both to the colonists to change their farming methods gradually and secure the means necessary to cultivate their lands by employing whites or freed blacks, and to the government time to reform the laws and policing system of the colonies. As a result of extending to the age of fifty the fertility span of slave women, and to sixty-five the life span of black males, there would be no slave left in the colonies in seventy years; the class of lifetime slaves would disappear in fifty years, and that of indentured slaves would be small and, finally, that at the end of thirty-five to forty years, the total number of slaves would have been reduced to zero,

while that of indentured Negro slaves would have come
down to, at most, a quarter of its current number.

Can anyone doubt that all this was done with the noblest
of intentions? But the world is full of wicked people who
should not be upset at any cost.

Condorcet—I have been quoting from his work[3]—found
the most appropriate words, the strongest expressions, to condemn slavery and not only demolish but, even better, ridicule
its legal and rational legitimacy, its moral bankruptcy, and
its economic and political opportuneness. Today's reader will
not know whose side to take. Should the reader let himself
be taken in by the mental high-wire gymnastics of the man
who, with the balancing pole of philosophy and colonialism
in his hands, is gingerly making his way over the hell of the
slave's daily life, his gaze fixed on that blessed horizon where
the sun will rise in seventy years? Or will the reader salute the
great courage of the man who told the slavers and all those
directly or indirectly associated with their frightful banditry
what they had to be told? Condorcet is categorical on this.
What I have discussed up to now is taken from chapter 9 of
his *Réflexions sur l'esclavage des nègres,* with its lovely sub-
title à la Montesquieu: *Des moyens de détruire l'esclavage des
nègres par degrés,* which concludes thus:

> What is proposed here is (i) to prevent the crimes of the
> masters by depriving them of an unjust right, or by enforc-
> ing the reparations stipulated by law; (ii) to let the masters
> enjoy their slaves for a period long enough to offset the costs
> incurred in buying and training them.[4]

Playing the quotation game? I realize that the compromises
of Condorcet—and of Raynal and Diderot—pale in comparison to their soulful laments on the fate of slaves, to their
flights of lyricism on the moral degeneracy of the masters.
Still, it is in those short concluding paragraphs that rhetoric

and anathemas yield their fundamental truths. A tree is recognized by its fruits,[5] and a theory judged by the practice to which it gives rise.[6]

The rhetoric of the Enlightenment and of the Revolution is worth absolutely nothing when judged against the only reality that matters: the master is guilty, the slave trade is a crime, slavery is the crime of all crimes: let's do away with it! Do away with it? Wait a moment! With some luck, thanks to the probity of the doctors who will palpate the bellies of "pregnant Negresses" and to the integrity of the inspectors who will distinguish in the mass of scars covering my body those inflicted on me by my master's whip from those caused by my clumsy handling of the sugarcane or resulting from knife fights on the plantations; to the reports of "young men who went to the colonies less to make a fortune than to satisfy their passion for study and for the sciences," it is at last possible that I might not spend a day—what am I saying?—not even an hour longer in slavery, seventy years after the auctioning of the *Code noir*.[7] And after they have gently and calmly taken care of me (unable, slave that I am, to take care of myself); after they have led me to discover natural human relations, about which I know nothing; after they have given me back this portion of my brain the gods took from me to make me endure slavery; after I have learned, without sulking, to respect my master and understood that under no circumstances am I to spit in his face; after they have lamented over sacrificing my inalienable rights (at least this is how they have been described) for the sake of the colony's well-being, since I could well take it over by killing and burning; when all these things have really come to pass, I shall eat from the hand of my master and mistress. Seventy years from now. They will give me a wage. I shall be free.

You can praise to high heavens the rigor of such and such a denunciation. You are entitled to find in the work of each of the men of the Enlightenment, emerging simultaneously into philosophy and politics, phrases and words that would be worthy of the contemporary antiracist slogan "hands off my pal." Yesterday's and today's antiapartheid activists could decorate their hats with them. Those who, today, here and there, must suffer in their bodies and souls for being what they are could well scribble them on their walls. But it will be wise and necessary for the historical record and even imperative for the sake of truth to follow the thread of the arguments and to pause on those passages that reveal the descent from such perceptive heights to the appalling rigor of ignoble compromises.

And what if, "all the while lamenting,"[8] Condorcet still chose the peace of sharks in opposing the immediate elevation of the slave to the realm of the human through the effective recognition of his rights; what if for his development he chose breeding and the barn at the expense of birth and being? I will be forgiven for not understanding, or for understanding only too well, why the progressive France of 1989 consecrated him by transferring his noble remains to the Panthéon. Could it be France's way of applauding—in these days of halftones and half measures, of pitiful confusion between the just and the unjust, between generosity and moneygrubbing—the fascinating beauty of compromise, the whorish excitement of consensus?

Am I straying off course? Let me come back, then, to the point. I realize that I am speaking of the most generous of all of them in talking about Condorcet. Let me emphasize in the strongest terms that I will not waste my time probing the depths of the discrepancy between the rhetoric and the "modalities of implementation" as others have dared to do—at least those who have deigned to look at the slave trade, to curse it, to cast an angry look at the colonists and a pitiful one on the slaves.

Corrupted by their masters, "the slaves in the European colonies have become incapable of carrying out normal human functions," wrote Condorcet. To whom shall they be compared? In relation to which law? To those whom society can consider as

> having lost their rights or as not having acquired them.
> Thus there are natural rights of which very young children
> are deprived as are madmen and idiots.

Slaves shall thus be considered for the moment, Condorcet continues,

> as men who have been deprived of some of their faculties
> through misfortune or illness, and who cannot be allowed
> the full exercise of their rights lest they harm others or
> themselves, and who therefore need not only the protection
> of the law but the caring of humanity.

Unless we are totally deluded, the decoded message is: slaves are not young children; they are idiots and madmen, dangerous to themselves and to others. That part of their brain that was excised by the gods will be given back to them when they have shown proof, seventy years from now, of their sociability and of a sufficient grasp of economic and social factors, of sound commonsense in the choice of what is urgent and what is not. We need to have them peaceful and thoughtful, free of bitterness and condescension. Three quarters of a century of preparation, then, to avert the danger that lies in wait for the sharks and that Condorcet describes in the severest of terms:

> If, however, the slightest certainty exists that a man is unfit
> to exercise his rights, and that if he is allowed such exercise
> of them, he will constitute a danger both to others and to
> himself, then society is entitled to regard that person as
> having lost his rights or as never having had them.

Who is outside the law here? The shark? Not at all. It is the black man. Now if I were a slave born in the Caribbean or abducted from Africa, I would ask myself a question that I would not dare ask my master for fear of the whip or the pillory: "Why, when it comes to me, am I kept outside the law, because of my vices and the danger that my accession to rights would pose to others, whereas in spite of their vices and crimes, I do not see my masters deprived of their rights?" The rest of Condorcet's answer clarifies what there is to be understood.

The perfect fit between the white man, irrespective of his shortcomings, and the model of the human that he has set up and that he protects by his laws is his good fortune. We know the black man's misfortune: he acquires his basic training outside the law, outside of humanity. He is supposed to acquire that which, elsewhere, is taken for granted.[9] On this score, it is worth pointing out that Condorcet does not add an iota to the laws in the *Code noir,* and also that I am in no way misrepresenting his thinking. I realize he states elsewhere that a society that tolerates injustice against any one of its members is no longer a society but an association of brigands. "The interests of the nation, both in terms of its power and wealth," he wrote in subtler and less radical words, "must give way to the rights of a single individual if there is to be a difference between a well-regulated society and a horde of thieves." More felicitously still he states:

> Any polity where general peace is secured through the viola-
> tion of the rights of its citizens or its foreigners ceases to be
> a society of human beings to become a den of thieves.

But is all this mere rhetoric, a slogan for a T-shirt, or is this applicable to law as it is experienced on a daily basis? And how does Condorcet apply these fine principles? By a clever mixture of the theoretical definition of what must be done and the translation of that definition into law in a manner consistent with Justice and Reason:

> The right to be protected by the forces of public safety
> against violence is one of the rights acquired by man upon
> entering society. The legislator thus owes it to society to

exclude all those who are foreign to it and liable to disrupt its peace. Unless he has taken adequate measures to anticipate and prevent trouble that, to his mind, could be triggered by his laws, and unless he has secured the force necessary to punish (without posing the least danger to the rest of the population) those who are guilty of fomenting it, the legislator owes it to society not to enact such laws, however just they may be. So, for example, before elevating slaves to the rank of freemen, the law must ensure that in their new estate these men do not pose a threat to public safety. The first step therefore is to recognize the danger to public order posed by the fury of masters wounded in their pride and avarice—for a man who has been used to seeing himself surrounded by slaves will not now be easily consoled by being surrounded by mere social inferiors. It is considerations such as these that can allow the legislator to defer, without committing a crime, the repeal of any law that deprives another man of his rights.

After these two paragraphs detailing Condorcet's thoughts on the phased abolition of slavery, how can one feel moved by the Enlightenment's unquestioned universal philanthropy and its equally unquestioned struggle for universal justice? What can one come up with that will not undermine the high-flown enthusiasm of the rhapsodists of our rational splendors?

The answer is quite simple. Let us put ourselves in the shoes of the real slave but at a safe distance from the whip. He asks for nothing. His human nature? He has been stripped of it, and in any case he is in no position to know what that is. His salvation? This is no business of his. The whites, with the *philosophes* at the forefront, are looking after it. How lucky. Stupid—Condorcet implies that much in his text—sometimes violent, he is liable to disrupt public order as soon as he is granted his freedom or, more precisely, as soon as (literally speaking) his chains are broken. Stupid and idiotic—sorry, but this is just an observation—he is capable on the eve of his emancipation, out of hatred for his master, of setting fire inadvertently to his cabin, of burning down the plantations out of spite, and of torching the homes of whites for the sheer fun of it. This would really be a shame. We will thus stagger the reparation of the injustice, the elimination of the genocide over time. We will need time to achieve these ends without provoking the fury of the colonists or damaging their interests—for the colonists, we know, are inconsolable once they are stripped of their slaves and "left with nothing but inferiors." Their greed and pride must be left undisturbed, their security guaranteed, even if this means suspending the promulgation of just laws.

We will keep all this in mind. We will be convinced of the sincerity and solidity of Condorcet's argument. We will be grateful to him for sketching out a gentle path from slavery to emancipation, a path that poses no threat to public order, to harvests, causes no panic to bankers or worry for Versailles (later the Republic) or fright in the navy, one that respects, above all, the anthropological hierarchy of rights dear to the Enlightenment, distinguishing between what is due the accomplished man and what is appropriate for individuals whose humanity continues to be problematic.[10] But what if the Enlightenment notion of justice is not seen to be applicable everywhere at the same time, if it rhymes with urgency in some places and parsimony in others? One can always extricate oneself from that problem with elegance and diplomacy, as the expression went: we will, lamenting all the while, make an appointment with history three-quarters of a century from now. Better still, we will revisit, without lamenting but with disquiet, the issue of urgency and parsimony if Toussaint Louverture seizes history by the scruff of the neck and hastens the rendezvous. Then we will use stronger language.

With these strong words on what must be done—and paying due regard to the demands of justice and the constraints of the calendar (how true that one cannot always do in this benighted

world what ought to be done and at the time when it should
be done)—Condorcet moves on to a new topic. He concludes
his chapter on "phased" emancipation and reflects on the economic advantages of employing free men rather than slaves on
the sugarcane, tobacco, indigo, and cotton plantations.

I am no longer interested, brainless slave that I am,[11] in the
calculations that now preoccupy the physiocrat,[12] however in-
sightful and clever they may be. I will leave that to the *philosophes* and the slave masters. I will judge the results from the
length of my working day, the bite of the whip or the softness
of the caress. I will be guided solely by what I become: free at
last or still enslaved, in spite of what they tell me. But I observe, with what little commonsense is left me, that in all this
palinode I am only discussed in relation to my ever-present
instincts, to a nature I am yet to discover, and to my litter that
I am to raise. Lacking in rights—only temporarily, I am told—
I wait to be humanized, to be whitened at last, so that I can as
a human being mind my own business. They have words for
that: civic life, politics, sovereignty, the body politic.

Alas, the slave has to realize one thing, namely, that his
long road to the rediscovery of human relations, the reclaim-
ing of his nature, can lead only to the threshold of rights and
not to rights themselves, to the precincts of the body politic
and not to the body politic itself. The reason is that lingering
doubt still remains, not on his ability to control his instincts
or to take care of his body and family (the latter being an extension of the former), but on his ability to contribute to the
running of the body politic, to whose influence he is already
subjected in his present animal state, should the master or
the body politic decide, at their discretion, to submit him to
its constraints.

Borrowing the language Las Casas imported into the Americas,[13] imposed there, and used as a calculated strategy in his
own struggles, I can say that Condorcet's Negro, the one raised
to be emancipated and taught to respect public order, is the

recognized carrier of a double sovereignty. As soon as he has discovered the relations befitting his nature and habits, he will find himself sovereign over himself as a human being (the monastic sovereignty of each to exercise dominion over himself), sovereign in the privacy of his home (the domestic sovereignty of the head of household). But what he cannot have is political sovereignty, neither for himself nor for his family. As members of a team of plantation workers (we're no longer speaking of slaves), his people make up no more than an indistinct mass, which is excluded from sharing political sovereignty.

Earlier, we caught our liberator dissociating, in the case of the slave masters, morality from legality from rights. You may be corrupt and corrupting, but you are not liable, from a strictly legal point of view, for impregnating Negresses or forcing them, as you deem fit, into prostitution. As masters, such conduct can only cheapen you; it cannot drag you down the ladder of civility. You are white. In you, as in the best theology of the Holy Trinity, the three sovereignties are irreducible one to the other. However, because you are neither a child, nor an idiot, nor a madman, they constitute an indivisible unity in your soul. Grow beyond childhood and you will discover that you are sovereign in the monastic, political, and domestic senses. You are white, and whites define sovereignty for themselves. Your possible turpitudes are examined case by case in light of "custom" and white law.

But be black and emancipated, and you will notice anthropology stuttering, as we saw earlier, logic rambling, and the Enlightenment vacillating. Where are you? Who are you? Do you really exist? You will see white generosity get a hold of itself and, having granted you the quality of being human, take it back, suddenly frightened by what, in a fit of daring, it had the nerve to do. It comes to its senses and puts you back in chains. It is in relation to you, and to you alone, that the question of the right to existence is raised through notions of doing and action—in a debate that generously seems to revolve around the question of your nature. From the answer, it will be concluded that either you are or you are not. Let us not prevaricate: you move from a state of simple nonexistence to some form of existence that remains a long way, a very long way, from a life of full legal and political rights. So do not nurse too many illusions about the radiant horizon at the end of the moratorium, for you may be disappointed, assuming your old, miserable bones can carry you that far.

Animal, We Will Give You a Soul

What is being planned for you? Condorcet explains. He imagines a master for whom kindness is not an empty word. One who, enriched from years of exploiting slaves on his (undoubtedly) prosperous plantations, suddenly gains enlightenment through some *philosophe.* Moved by the latter's message, the master suddenly sees the horror of the slavery by which he has hitherto grown fat, and, Condorcet continues,

> considering the happiness of the slaves as his supreme duty, and the loss of their liberty and rights as an evil it behooves him to correct, he rushes to his plantations to shed his tyrannical ways, to don the authority of the just and humane sovereign to commit himself to making humans beings out of his slaves. He trains them to become industrious workers and intelligent farmers. Hope of legitimate profits and the desire to make his family happier would be the sole motives for his work. Punishment that in the past resulted from greed and caprice is now reserved only for crimes; it is determined by judges chosen from among fellow Negroes. The vices of the slaves would disappear with those of the master. Soon the master finds himself among friends who are passionately and heroically attached to him. He shows that the most fertile lands are not necessarily those that are

cultivated by the most miserable of slaves, and that man's true happiness need not be bought at the expense of that of his brothers. The crack of the whip and the howling of slaves give way to the sweet, tender flute music of the banks of the Niger. Instead of servile fear, as humiliating to its recipient as it is revolting to the one causing it; instead of this picture of servitude, ferocity, prostitution, and misery to which the master's presence has put an end, the master sees springing all around him the rustic but innocent simplicity of patriarchal life. The moving sight of happy families united in work and recreation strikes him. Honesty, love of virtue, maternal and filial love—all these tender emotions, enriching the life of these unfortunate people—become the fruit of his labor. And instead of growing rich from the misfortune of his slaves, he finds bliss in their happiness.[14]

If I were a slave, I could not help but notice the insulting sarcasm of this speech, a speech that I should read, I imagine, in tears, delighted and fascinated with the depth and intensity of the good that is wished for me. I am told that from the slave that I am, I will be made into a human being. Should I rejoice as the latest invective against slavery—now condemned as dehumanizing—whistles past my ears? Or should I worry about what is coming next?

True, I will now have a right to my own police, since I shall have been invited to choose the color of my judges (is it really their color?). But will I really need to choose them? Coming from the nothingness of slavery, my vices are really not mine. They are but acts of imitation of my master, who alone can, of his own accord, do good or evil. Now since I am dealing with a master who is a model of virtue, I become human through my contact with him and have therefore no need for judges! Was I violent, miserable, and vile? My good master's presence will bring me to that original simplicity that suits my needs, to the patriarchal system of those who know what a cabin or bed is but do not know what the body politic is. Within that system, I will go to bed with my Negress and impregnate her. With our little black children, we will all work very hard for the good master, for my "just and humane sovereign," for this white man who has suddenly given up tyranny and discovered authority, for this slaver who has been made sovereign by philosophy. At night my entire brood, my wife and I, will rest, our duties done.

The master has transformed me into a human being. I really was not one, neither in his eyes nor, deep down, in Condorcet's. I was, on my own, incapable either of vice or virtue. I was nothing but dust, dirt, and waste. A Negress? I had to be a prostitute. There was no doubt about that. For it is the master, and he alone, who can instill in me sentiments that I had no idea existed. Honesty, virtue, maternal and filial love? I did not know all that existed. From time immemorial, as the slavers had said, all I did was lie and betray. Poison and arson? That is my name. Rape? That is me again. And how about stealing? Of course, I steal everywhere: in the house and on the plantations. I steal from blacks, cheat whites, poison everyone, have sex left and right. Never have I shown the least bit of inclination for mercy. Do I look like someone who can be moved by the plight of his own brothers and sisters? Have I ever been seen to hesitate from knocking down a weak, limping old man? Even when I have eaten my full, have I ever been seen resisting the temptation of stealing a hungry child's gruel? Virtue? I have no idea what that is. Never have I tempered the misfortune of any of my brothers with mercy, pity, or friendship. Anyway, do I even have any idea of the notion of brother, ignorant as I am of natural human relations?

I was expelled at a very early age from the bosom of my whorish mother, who did not abort me on account of exhaustion or forgetfulness. And I saw her scamper with joy, wriggle her hips in a frantic and obscene fit of female laughter when— after I was sold off to another master—she realized, in her instinctive animal way, that she would never see me again, but concluded that it was good riddance for the two of us. We black children have always hated our parents as intensely as they have cursed us. But Condorcet reassures me. All these crimes were not really crimes. I could not help being what I was. My coarse "simplicity" suited less my slave situation than it did my bestial nature. As for my soul, the good master will adorn it with tender and generous sentiments and even more. But Condorcet smoothes over his blunder: a nonexistent soul cannot be adorned. It has to be created beautiful, in one's own image—"their soul would be his product." The master, whose slave I no longer am, endows me with a soul. The gods can from now on restore the stolen half of my brain.

This, then, is where Condorcet leads the slave: to the acquisition of a soul that, by association, is graced with basic virtues; to the use of a flute on the banks of the Niger; to a renunciation of the usual howling; higher still: to a heroic faithfulness to his lord and master, his true creator.

And I am expected after all this to strut with satisfaction! How can I for a moment be happy with a discourse that is so shocking in the way it legitimizes the most cruel slavers as it describes me, out of goodness of heart, mercy, and pity,[15] in exactly the same way as it would out of greed, indifference, and self-interest.

This condescending slide down the abyss of nothingness, which stands in as nature for me, can be explained. It partakes of a terribly cold logic. There is an insurmountable barrier between domestic and political sovereignty, which it is highly urgent to preserve. For no reason in the world must the "coarse but innocent simplicity of patriarchal life" be allowed to be converted into subtle and calculated claims on, or an appropriation of, that sovereignty. The "tender looks" of the good, condescending master must not turn into the anguished vigilance of the trapped master, tangled up with his slaves. We play the fife, Condorcet-like, in the master's plantation but not the drum that brings together men desirous of claiming their share of power. That transition from fife to drum is nowhere envisaged in Saint Condorcet's work. Let it be said in passing that Raynal and Diderot "playing the drums" here and there,[16] in Mercier's footsteps,[17] makes me sick—privy as I am to their dealings with Versailles and various shipping companies, and to their dividends. But let me return, suitably purged, to Condorcet. Is the transition from fife to drum, or before that from "howls" to drum, at least mentioned in his work? It certainly is. But it is barely mentioned before it is warded off in the name of his Highness Public Order, a concern that is none of my business from the very first day I start receiving humanitarian care up to, if my understanding is correct, the last evening before the dawn of the end of the moratorium. As a good reader of Montesquieu, Condorcet is satisfied with mercy and pity, postponing, while lamenting, the implementation of justice that he now defines as sovereign authority, and with which he replaces, under the pleasant tropical sun, the master's tyranny.

Nothing, it will be agreed, is less neutral in the discourse of the Enlightenment than the meaning of terms such as *tyranny* or *master* or *sovereign* or *authority* or *patriarchal style* or *ingenuousness* or *social or civil behavior.* Among Enlightenment thinkers in general, and the authors of the *Encyclopédie* in particular, these terms point to different conceptions of human nature and of the state of being of society in one or another of its different stages: either from the unveiling of the nature of the group to itself, up to the stage of civilized polity that determines its meaning, or from the growing perfection of the nature of man or the gradual unveiling of its sudden and founding accomplishment—from the pre-history of the contract to the flourishing or the crisis of this very civilized polity.

Condorcet, more than any other thinker, fails to envisage full political sovereignty for Negroes. He stops at patriarchal happiness for them, granting them political rights only when they cease to be Negroes. The *Réflexions* are unequivocal on this point. But it should also be remembered that bearing in mind the proportion of few whites to many blacks in the Caribbean, especially in Saint-Domingue, Condorcet foresaw a trend in miscegenation that pointed not to the darkening of whites but to the whitening of blacks. He explains:

> There will necessarily be in each colony, initially, two types of people, whose food, customs, and traditions will differ. After a few generations, the blacks will merge with the whites to a point where the only difference left will be that of color. But the mixture of races will eventually lead to the disappearance of even this last difference.

Clearly, what one has here is a process of cultural whitening first, to be followed by the disappearance pure and simple of black modes of behavior, modes that will be indistinguishable from those of whites. It is unclear to me how, from Condorcet's perspective, such miscegenation will lead to a greater darkening rather than a whitening of the population. I do not wish to quibble, like the Spanish did at the time, about the shades of blackness or whiteness in each individual.[18] As a slave, I will, however, remember that nothing is given to me in the realm of politics, since I give up customs and practices and am not responsible for the law. By the same token, I will discover that behind this way of making the gods responsible for my inhuman condition lurks a definition of my humanity that has more in common with the pre-contractarian Hobbes—petulant, vociferous, and murderous—than with the pre-contractarian Rousseau—carefree, tender, and compassionate.[19]

But I am straying off course again. I am blinded by "negritude" and slavery. I cannot, without pettiness, spend so much time showing the duplicity embedded in so much goodness. I cannot claim to bring out the dark side of the Enlightenment at the point when, humanizing me as a slave, it adorns my mind with its brilliance. Have I ever been told that I deserve everything, I who am deprived of everything, even of myself?

The reason is that the Enlightenment has not decided very firmly. It dabbles in the non-negotiable, cheapens what it adores, displays for auction on the steps of the temple that against which its anathema should be directed, upholds slavery even as it condemns it, maintains servitude even as it ridicules it, extols submissiveness and yet glorifies revolt, crushes liberty at the same time as it celebrates it. What did the Enlightenment bring to the world, this world that sustains us both, master and slave? Is it the beaconlike notion that man has mastery over his body, that he is sovereign over himself, that he enjoys free will? The world knew this long before the Enlightenment came along to crack the black vault of the sky of prejudice or, to borrow its language, to undo the harm caused by the "knowledge" of the ignorant and by the "science" of the theologians. That "the Englishman's home is his castle" is something the Englishman did not need to be told, even when he wore neither gloves nor wig. The Enlightenment neither invented the notion of political sovereignty nor the idea of the individual exercise of that sovereignty. That was well known. An Andalusian bishop had known it for at least two centuries.[20] And that he knew it was a well-known fact. Each individual partakes of that sovereignty, wrote the old bishop as far back as 1519: "There is not, and there cannot exist, a population that is not a people; and there is not, and there cannot exist a people that is not sovereign." The idea of political sovereignty as an attribute of each individual was well known before the Enlightenment. What is true is that the Enlightenment went a step further and imposed this idea without hooking it, as does Spinoza, to some sort of gradation or alchemy (known only to four initiates, or is it two?) in the ability to distinguish between the duty to act from knowledge and the right to act from sentiment or passion.[21] It was emphatic, refusing to make sovereignty the privilege of some over here and the regret of others over there.

But I, a slave, am neither from here nor from elsewhere. I am from nowhere. I do not count. The Enlightenment and Condorcet, more than most of its thinkers, have elevated me to the same heights on which the priests had already placed me. No, I am not a monkey. I am a human being.[22] I am a human being capable of good and evil, of evil especially. I am supposed to cherish my companion hitherto a monkey but now recognized as a woman, to feed my children at my pleasure, in my own good time, to my satisfaction. I am unfit to be counted among humans when they assemble under clear sky to play the grand game of their collective sovereignties.

But let my people assemble. Let them simply attempt to show themselves within cannon range of the agora where the sovereign people are meeting to legislate—where men are busy with their affairs and guarding the peace of their home; let me dare go there, me a freed black, a slave, an animal, a human being for almost a thousand moons, and I will be noisily and duplicitously chased back to the "unpolitical" nothingness of my bestiality.

Is that all? I am made an extra, a mute extra in the grandiose theater of their tribunals, on the express condition that, grateful to the point of tears for their largesse, I play them the fife. I am accepted in their assemblies when, through their infinite kindness, I first whiten up my ways, then my grimaces, and finally my skin. Black, now you are white. You may come in and legislate with us.

Did Condorcet require similar sacrifices of Jews and women? Where, if anywhere, does he write: "Jew, you are now a Christian; come in and legislate" or "Woman, now you are a man; come in and legislate"? Would it not be absurd, insulting, unacceptable for Jews and women? And yet, when it is "black man you are white," it is supposed to be a grandiose act of philanthropy and fraternity for me as well as for my poor, colored, and derelict brothers.

No, I am not off course. I read, and I can read. That is my

job. I do not doubt Condorcet is lamenting when he says so. I am not for one moment questioning his good intentions. I am not so foolish as not to admit that his criticism of slavery works in his favor. All I do is observe this massive piece of evidence, of patriarchal evidence, if you will—the fact that he, like others, during the Enlightenment at its most productive and influential moments upheld Montesquieu's proposition: justice and rights in nations and for men, but for me and my kin "pity and mercy." Have pity and mercy, indeed, and stop subjugating my enslaved or emancipated brain to the fiery declarations of those who took on my cause, even as they received profits from slavers, or of those who point to my distress as just one instance among many of man's tragic condition in the twilight of the eighteenth century. My situation is totally different. Do you doubt this? Well, let us agree to meet in court; let us walk there together, if you can endure the company of a Negro slave or of one who is in the process of being freed or has only recently been freed.

We have just learned that the Negro, endowed with a soul entirely created for him by the white man, can choose the judges that will have to punish him for his crimes. But let us also forget that we learned simultaneously that this would be pure luxury, given the type of soul with which the black man will be endowed. No doubt, it is a substantial gift that Condorcet gives to the freed slave. But who is this black man who can now elect his judges? Is he the one who moves imperceptibly from slavery to freedom through a long moratorium, or is he the one whose master, suddenly enlightened by philosophy, becomes a sovereign rather than a master? It is the latter and not the former. The latter, with the white soul, chooses his judge; we already noted that seeing the constraints of the context, the exercise was not worth it, but never mind. The former, the slave who has gone through the moratorium, chooses nothing and in fact does not even have legal abilities. Mute in front of the judge, mute he remains in Condorcet's

Réflexions, and mute he is in the *Code noir,* which states in article 30:

> Slaves cannot hold offices or mandates that involve the discharge of any public functions; they cannot be made agents, for the running or management of a business, by anyone other than their masters; neither can they sit as arbitrators, experts, or witnesses in civil or criminal cases. In cases where their testimony is heard, it can only be used to refresh the memory of the judges; it cannot provide the basis for any assumptions, conjectures, or proof.

Lest some fanciful retort to this be brought up, let us look at article 31:

> A slave cannot be party to, or be judged in, a civil matter either as plaintiff or defendant nor can he institute a criminal action in his own right in redress of a wrong against him; only his master acting as his next friend in a civil matter can seek reparations, in a criminal matter, for outrages and excesses committed against the slave.

But public order has to be respected! The slave must also have a place in the theater of justice. Well, he has it. It is described very well in article 32:

> Criminal proceedings can be instituted against slaves without involving their masters, except in cases of complicity. Said slaves can be judged on first hearing by ordinary judges and on appeal by a sovereign council, following the same rules and formalities used for free men.

It is difficult to imagine that this remarkable physiocrat, the last of the great *Encyclopédistes,* could have been totally unaware of the *Code noir* and its import. It is out of the question that this generous and courageous man—several times president of the "Friends of Blacks"—would not have reflected at length on the philosophical and anthropological ramifications of the idea of the competence or incompetence before the law of the slave who is in the process of being freed. "The slaves in the European colonies have become incapable of fulfilling their functions as free men." This position of Condorcet's we already knew. We also knew that "a sense of natural relations either does not exist or has been corrupted in the slave, and that emotions natural to man are similarly not experienced by him or have been smothered by oppression." In sum, we knew that it was by taking all this into account that the slaves would be taken care of in a manner that did not "expose them to the risk of harming others or themselves."[23] Is anything else needed to block their path—obviously in their interests—to legal competence? These important observations of short-comings, of fundamental shortcomings, in the law largely suffice. And we find Condorcet as generous in denying access to legal rights to the slaves that he is humanizing (all the while lamenting), as was the *Code noir* without lamenting.

A passage suddenly states that "it is at eighteen that male or female children of slaves in perpetuity would be given the right to bring criminal proceedings against a master for personal injury (. . .) Each colony or canton shall have a public official with the sole responsibility of defending blacks," one of whose tasks would be to "charge the masters when, and if, it is proved to that official's satisfaction that the masters' crimes have not been sufficiently punished by freeing these indentured children." This is wonderful. This Negro "ombudsman" would radically change the situation from that described in the *Code noir*.[24] Here, at least, the young Negro ("the child") can speak; he can press legal charges and secure punishment, if appropriate. This is a decidedly new proposal, a skillful way of cracking the door open on the issue of the incapable Negro's competence. Can I nonetheless compare these measures to the substance of the useless article 26 of the *Code noir*, two or three of whose provisions—30 and 31—previously cited, cynically nullify these effects? I will take the liberty of quoting article 26 in its entirety for the reader's close attention:

> Slaves who have not been fed, clothed, and maintained by their masters according to the said rules could notify the prosecutor and provide him with information that could be used immediately, if corroborated with testimonies from elsewhere, to prosecute masters at the slaves' request and with no costs to them. We would like to see these measures observed for crimes and barbaric and inhuman treatment of slaves by their masters.

After which, I must point out that it is Condorcet himself who notes very correctly that no master was ever punished for crimes committed against the bodies (can one say "the person"?) of slaves.[25] And I can conclude from this that if in the *Code noir* articles 31 and 36 take away all the credibility of article 26, I got a much better deal in Condorcet's proposals. Unless, of course, I conclude, after reading them closely, that it is impossible to summarize them neatly and so find myself painfully obliged, once again, to quote from them at length. This is unavoidable:

> A man who would have had his Negroes tortured, who would have had them slowly burnt, deserves a punishment other than [the freeing of his slaves]: now to inflict these types of punishment on him, it is not enough to establish them by law; the crime has to be proved. Would it be just in such cases to admit the testimony of slaves against their masters? Some propagandists may think so. They would say "Masters have no right to own slaves. Such ownership is only permissible on the condition that if they are accused of a crime by one of their slaves, they can be condemned through the testimony of the others. It is to keep the right so dear to them to freely violate all the laws of nature that they expose themselves to no longer observe the precautions that

are laid down by the law to protect the liberty of the citizens. Let them free their slaves; let them be just, and society will be just with them." It can be objected to such reasoning that not only is the law unjust—and this judgment derives from our firmly established principles [that slavery in itself is a crime on the part of the master]—but that such injustice will strengthen the slaves in their vices. On the other hand, if the testimony of slaves is not admitted, then any proof of crimes committed by the master becomes impossible to establish—from whence it can be concluded that in any permanent state of servitude, there is no just and legal way of providing for the security of the slaves.

What place does the generous Condorcet provide in court for the freeable slave, where the *Code noir* slams the door in his face? Who in the end—in Condorcet's scheme of things—will bear witness to the torture inflicted on me or on one of my brothers? Condorcet values my virtue far too much to contemplate without shuddering the risk that, as a witness, I might lay it on too thick, and that, as a victim, I may exaggerate things. I must therefore keep quiet. Who is to witness then? The answer is simple: the inspector, the doctor! "An ordinary inspection," "the doctor's opinion" and the matter is settled without the hilarious risk of encouraging the vices of the slaves, their abnormal taste for lies. I should have thought of this earlier since, after all, it is among inspectors and doctors that "lies the hope of finding humanity, justice, and morality in the colonies."

So the reality of torture, the cruelties and crimes of the white masters are finally left to the kind discretion of the doctor and the inspector, also white. What is at stake here is the curbing of the vices of the slaves, the safeguarding of the smallest flowering of the smallest seed of virtue in the slave. What is at stake here is public order and the prestige of the law. And our noble montage will function by riveting the Negro to his incapacity. Thank you Condorcet. The *Code noir* with the panache of its perfect monstrosity said as much.

What should I, a slave, take away from Condorcet's long-winded prevarications, from the tangled positions of a man who, as a good physiocrat, is mindful to the point of ridicule of public order, the profitability of the colonies, and the economic status quo—if not for the manner of production, then at least for the results and dividends?

Do I have a soul that has been generously given to me and that I display at will before the judges? Am I so perverse that my testimony about what is done to my body, or what I see done in the plantation where I labor cannot be accepted, as was the case in the *Code noir*? All this because I am a compulsive liar who perversely aims at only one thing: to obtain the unjust condemnation of my tyrant? What is the law for me? The result of self-denial? Do I have to become a model of heroic virtue—and how could I?—for my Negro humanity to merit that which the torturer's humanity possesses without anyone ever thinking of divesting him of it? Or am I so threatening in my misery, in spite of my undeniable stupidity, so dangerous in my bestiality that Condorcet fears that if I am allowed to address the court, the tribunal will explode from the force of my roar?

So I am denied access to the law. What is left for me are the subterfuges of the regulations, which I can use to my advantage at the pleasure of a few generous souls but not as a matter of right. A few souls, not many. And Condorcet wonders further down whether he could find "twelve or so" noble souls in whom to entrust the scales and the sword of that "justice."

Should I shed tears over this? Laugh over it? Neither reaction is probably necessary. But it is urgent, it seems to me, not to cheat and to realize what exactly we celebrate in France when we celebrate wildly the enormous force and wonderful egalitarianism of our universal philanthropy and what is left of it after our compromises with the cult of justice.

One more detail on the question of the relationship of the Negro to his rights before moving on to other calamities: Toward the end of the chapter on his "Proposals to Ease the Enslavement of Negroes," Condorcet makes the point even more forcefully. He envisages, at the same time as he is warding it off, a technique of "open prevarication on the part of the judges," one whose effect would be to neutralize completely the transitional laws regulating slavery and emancipation during the moratorium. This general prevarication, both envisaged and fended off, will not happen. Should some colonists keep freed slaves? That would be a crime, but that crime "can be proved legally without recourse either to the testimony of blacks or to the depositions—even more suspect—of whites." Black slave that I am, I clearly do not know what to make of this mental alchemy according to which I cannot be a witness (Condorcet forbids me that) although I know, thanks to Condorcet, that I am a "free black."

In search of my political sovereignty, I hung around in the shadows close to the tribunal to observe. It is more and more clear to me that the only appropriate response to all the insolent questions that I have dared ask about my condition has already been given. I am nothing legally and politically. I am not like them. Will seventy years be enough for me to tear myself from my stupidity and my vices and to cultivate virtue to a point elevated enough for their nature? Such are the stakes. Such is the cruel and ridiculous mercy of the Enlightenment.

Seventy years. And why not immediately? Each and every single one of Condorcet's contradictions in *Réflexions* can be reduced to one: that slavery must be rigorously and, to be redundant, completely managed, at the same time as its consequences are eased and its end is programmed. It took, as we know, the explosion of Saint-Domingue for the nonsense of all this humanitarianism to be exposed, and for people to realize that there are no two ways between slavery and freedom, bestiality and humanity: you seize all of one when you are strong enough to tear yourself free from all of the other. But, of course, such an operation can only be accomplished by radically changing the content of the notion of "public order." It is what the slaves of Saint-Domingue will do. And this is what Condorcet could never bring himself to imagine.

Ham's Time. Shem's Love. Japheth's Goodness

So the moratorium. Unavoidably. The alternative invented by Condorcet is clear: either the progressive disappearance of slavery, or slavery in perpetuity. To the extent that Versailles declared its support for the easing of the conditions of the slave, Condorcet's position was consistent with Versailles' political will and with that of the authorities of his day. He differed from it, however, in his vision of a liberating end. But, as we have already observed, he insisted above all on the maintenance of public order, of this order that must lead—it is promised— blacks and whites to the harmonious conviviality some of whose sweet rhythms we have already heard.

The one-sidedness is unmistakable: the slave has conceded all that must be conceded to injustice. The master must understand, and Condorcet is at pains to explain to him that he stands to gain everything and lose nothing the moment when, complying with the measures worked out for the complete duration of the moratorium, he transitions imperceptibly from the employment of slave labor to that of wage labor. Will the masters open their ears? Will they listen to reason? Condorcet has no doubt they will. Will they do everything to neutralize the beneficial results of the moratorium and maintain at all cost the unbridled power that they have been used to? The encyclopedist's wager on this crucial issue is of angelic innocence.

Knowing that the laws easing the harshness of slave conditions are necessarily temporary—since their ultimate objective is the emancipation of all and the disappearance of slavery—pedagogy will work its effect. If, on the other hand, the metropole proposed reforms—even the overhaul—of the *Code noir,* real improvements in the condition of slaves, ever-greater possibilities for emancipation but without envisaging an end to slavery, the colonists would beat the laws and the legal system, as they do today. They therefore readily listen to all that they are told about the need to reform the *Code noir* (some even pitch in with their plans), knowing fully well what little importance they would attach to these reforms. They will know how to put these and other future changes to their advantage. And the slave in the islands will continue to moan just as much as he did in the past, irrespective of the comfort that the conscience of whites in France will take from reading a collection of laws that is better than that of 1686. In a word, Condorcet's bad laws are better because the legalization of injustice that they promote is by definition obsolete.

Let us forget for a moment what we know about the effectivity of the sovereignty of the Negroes at the end of the moratorium, and take Condorcet on his word: the alternative is either, and here I am rambling a bit, liberty for all in seventy years or no liberty ever. And this is grounded on one and only one criterion: the opinion of the colonists. At bottom, one and only one criterion counts: the profitability of the colonies, which presupposes the ability of the colonists to understand where their interests lie. Taking one imperative into account nevertheless: from rooftops and in page after page, it is proclaimed loud and clear that it would be a disgrace to compensate the thief for the legal confiscation of his spoils. It is noted that the colonist stole the slave that he subjugates, whether that slave was born in his country or bought in the market. It is made clear, however, that the master is entitled to the labor of his slave up to the slave's thirty-fifth year as compensation for his cost at the fair or his upbringing in the fields or on the plantation.[26]

The conditions and consequences of a general emancipation are undoubtedly examined at the appropriate moment. The title of chapter 8, where they are sketched out, spares no surprises. It is a "no," "no" to general emancipation, and this is its title: "Examination of the Reasons That Can Prevent the Legislature of States That Tolerate the Enslavement of Blacks from Fulfilling, through a Law of General Emancipation, the Duty to Justice That Obliges That State to Grant Them Their Freedom." Reasons are given, but whatever the grandiloquence of the text, they boil down to three.

The first: for the freed slave not to go from slavery to misery, a number of temporary supporting measures need to be put in place—for food aid and general assistance to the liberated mass, care to the young and the elderly, and compensation to the victims of judicial . . . excesses. The masters will not want to take that responsibility, and the legislature, out of concern above all for public order, cannot force them to do that. If the government shoulders that responsibility, "it would increase the burden of taxation on the innocent in order to spare the guilty." Conclusion: the plan is too expensive and therefore unrealizable.

The second: the freed blacks cannot be contained like whites by "the same laws." They will assemble, steal, rape, commit acts of targeted revenge, and roam the mountains and forests. The whites will secretly stir up trouble to have slavery reestablished. Quite clearly the blacks, infinitely more numerous than the whites, would seize power, which they will exercise with no regard for their oppressors. Gone, in that case, will be public order, gone the colony. It is therefore unacceptable.

The third: the stupidity of the slaves, their degradation, corruption, ignorance of natural relationships, which although the fault of the masters, nonetheless remains a fact. But the question rings out: "Are these people worthy of being entrusted with their happiness and the responsibility of their families?" The answer: they are not. "In that case whatever the reasons that may have made them unfit to be human, what the laws owe them is less their rights than their well-being."

Strengthened by these considerations, which boil down to one, namely, that the order that the slaves will establish is intolerable to the interests of whites and the continued existence of the colony, Condorcet concludes: "These are the reasons that have led us to believe that the decision not to grant to all the slaves the enjoyment of their rights all at once need not be incompatible with justice."

Condorcet is really not speaking rashly when he insists on my inhumanity even as he identifies the person responsible for the dehumanization of the slave. For throughout the *Réflexions,* he continuously refers, in order to bring out their disadvantages, to the thousand and one instruments of coercion that governments have at their disposal to control the colonists and force some humanity on them. But any form of coercion of the colonist that is too flagrant endangers what he produces, and runs the risk of signaling the beginning of the end of the colony, of dealing a severe blow to French trade, which is jealous of its monopoly. Can one do any better to safeguard the slaver and the slave trade?

On the other hand, the idea that I can establish my order (which you describe at will as plunder, vagrancy, bestiality) on the land where I was thrown up by your people, or where I was born, grew up, and developed in spite of you is intolerable to you and all the *philosophes* of your neighborhood. Your considerations that "I am not yet fully human," "I am not yet ready" to take care of my pleasure and happiness, of my family and my hammock are all excuses! Condorcet knows how to read and research a topic, and he does his research. He is very expert at inducing and deducing. If my history begins with the fire of Saint-Domingue, he knows how many tragic and aborted births preceded this painful birth. In short he knows very well that master in my home, a citizen in my city, a member and integral part of my community, I just might make it clear to those concerned, through cannon fire, that the law is henceforth me, us. Not him, not them. It is therefore necessary—the ploy is so obvious—that I not be considered human, whoever is responsible for my bestiality, in order to give France the time to supervise my humanization at the same time as it improves the colonial economy and its productivity.

Do it all gently; the slavers will not understand any rush. Implement it imperceptibly, with no shocks, lest the oppressors raise eyebrows. So let's leave the moratorium to bear fruit. Soon the music of flutes from the banks of the Niger will cradle us during siesta. Let us rush nothing. It takes time to make a soul for a person who has none and to breathe it into his body. But it is pleasant. Try and you will see. Divide your huge plantations into smaller farms, gentlemen slavers. And you will discover that "by sticking to the slow pace of emancipation that we proposed to you," your losses, dear citizens, will be as gradual and minimal as you can imagine. And who is talking about losses? Calculate with me, and you will see that you need have no worries. Look. "Most of the freed slaves would be cheaply hired, since most of them can only be employed in agriculture and, in any case, no more than as day laborers whose wage for this same reason will not exceed the basic minimum." Thank you Saint Condorcet. I am worth nothing, it is now perfectly clear. Sudden emancipation from nothing at the risk of new taxes on those poor people; unheard of banditry for the pleasure of a band of animals—this is frankly "impolitic," as they say. But wait a minute . . . You did say, didn't you, that born in the slaver's house I will only be free at thirty-five, and that my years of labor in slavery would compensate my master for the cost of my education and upbringing? Yes, that is what you said, I remember. It was again for public consumption, wasn't it? My master fed me, if you say so—it is extremely rare for the farmer to starve to death a calf that he wants to raise as a draft ox—but he taught me nothing! And now you point out to my brutal oppressor, transformed by your laws into my just sovereign (the words, Marquis, are yours, not mine), that at bottom he can pay me whatever he chooses for a day's work in the fields, and that it is either that or nothing because after all anyone can do my job. And for you to deserve the Pantheon two centuries later for having promoted me after a moratorium of sixty years from nothingness to worthlessness is a good deal, your holiness, you must admit.

And since you have decided to mix my destiny, which is of such concern to you, with that of the Jews, who are infinitely more indebted to you than I am,[27] permit me to visit those areas where you have unwisely handled the encounter between the sons of Shem and of Ham, to talk like people did under the streaming rays of the Enlightenment sun. What have the Jews got to do with your indecent moratorium? Well, here is the explanation: they come to the plantations hand in hand with the Protestants to rebuild their civic and economic life, all the while taking part in the march toward my emancipation, whose slow pace you have deemed compatible with justice or—what basically amounts to the same thing—with a gross injustice that justice would tolerate.

Whether the Protestants acquire plantations there, whether they buy them here and there, or by cantons, whether they employ a hundred men, whites or blacks, but free (do they free them on buying them, or do they only use free labor?), or freely practice their religion, which the *Code noir* does not want to hear about in the tropics, so much the better for them. In the same breath, the Jews will be lavishly compensated over there, in the islands, for the discriminations they endemically suffer here, in France. They could acquire plantations on the same terms extended to Protestants. They would leave in droves. The poor Jews, "naturally austere and thrifty," will not be averse to cultivating as free men the lands on which the rich Jews would have settled them. The rich Jews would "share

the produce" with the poor ones. But will the rich Jews be sufficiently attracted by this offer "to own real landed property"?
Condorcet has no doubt about it, and he adds:

> To increase the incentives, they would only be obliged to
> free, each year, a sixth of the slaves held in perpetual or
> temporary bondage that they find in already established
> plantations. By this is meant a sixth of the number of active
> male or female slaves, that would be on a plantation the first
> year, each family bringing with it its children above fifteen.
> Through this method, the emancipation will be faster still,
> and at the same time the owner will be given added interest
> to keep his slaves since all the dead would amount to a pure
> loss for him.

From my perspective as a slave, I must admit that this is a
fascinating tactic: transforming the end of my interminable
Calvary into the slope on which the Protestant will slide
down to recover all his rights—rights that I did not despoil
him of—and the Jew the exercise of the sacred right of ownership of land that I did not deprive of either. A little while ago,
when Condorcet dismissed the idea of the immediate emancipation of all my people, he explained movingly that such
emancipation would increase the burden of taxation on the
innocent in the metropole who cannot be held responsible for
the problem. And what about me, I wonder? Am I responsible for the revocation of the Edict of Nantes? Am I responsible for the dark hours of the destiny of Shem?[28] And why,
for goodness sake, for which rewards or in the expiation of
which crimes must I, a poor slave, endure an extension (and
by how many years, this one?) of my seventy-year moratorium, so that the Jews, poor or rich alike, but "naturally" hard-
working and thrifty, may discover the pleasure of ownership
of land? Am I really that stupid as Condorcet says? Certainly
not to the point of being unable to detect in the mathematics
of this emancipatable "sixth" of my people—a figure adjusted

by the expression "active"—the dawn of a new moratorium whose end this godly man forgets to schedule. Pathetic Enlightenment, a robber's fair, a quarrel of vultures in jabots, an exemplary disgrace. Condorcet, the sworn anticlericalist, the man whom the fate of papists on the stake does not move any less than that of the Catalonian Servet or members of his faith,[29] suddenly remembers, at my expense, that of my suspect humanity and of my certain stupidity, that he once read first in the Bible, then in Montesquieu,[30] something relating to Jewish practices of enslavement and emancipation. And he applies all that to me, enlivening his act with some expression about my "conservation" and death, which a pig or cattle farmer would use with as much elegance and relevance.

What! Our "pantheonized" encyclopedist wittily ironizes about the clause in the *Code noir* that stipulates that children inherit the status of their mother and not their father: to a slave mother, a slave son, to a free mother free, a free son![31] The *Code noir* is implicitly referring, in order to spell it out more clearly, to the Roman law that stipulates that the "offspring follows the womb" ("partus sequitur ventrem"). Condorcet explodes: "It is strange, perhaps, that a tyrannical law, made by brigands on the banks of the Tiber, renewed by a courtesan's husband on the banks of the Propontis, should still be causing the misery of people in the seas of America two hundred years later." But at the very moment that he is inviting Jews to the feast, he surreptitiously slides in the "law of the sixth," a clear reference to the sabbatical emancipation—how many years old, your Marquis?—so that Shem should have no hesitation to feed off the fruits of the tree watered by the blood and tears of the slave, Ham!

To bring to a close the bicentennial celebrations of what it began in 1789, France "pantheonized" the man—enormously meritorious in other respects—who out of virtue, and moaning, but fully in tune with the inconsistencies of the anthropology of the Enlightenment, condemned me again on appeal to slavery, me Ham the beast, for the good looks of Shem whose humanity, luckily, was never in doubt. How nice.

It is also nice to witness the petulance of these *philosophes* and encyclopedists as they ferret under cover of darkness, on the sly, in the shadows, bits and pieces from the scrap heap of rusty metal in the bottomless pit of bigotry, filing and oiling them, repairing them and fitting them into the brilliant clockwork machinery of the Enlightenment so that it can tick flawlessly in the interests of white papists, Jews, and their coreligionists whose elevation from a state of subjection to the king to citizenship with full legal and property rights is the concern here. If an old Biblical law that has been obsolete can come in handy, at both ends of tradition, to Montesquieu's show of elegance and scruples, why deprive oneself of it? I, Ham, am ordered by the Enlightenment to wait that I be humanized while Japheth decides, if luck is on my side, on the number of years that Shem will think it necessary to add to the process.

Condorcet is right. It is impossible and impolitic to grant immediate freedom to all? That is impossible and impolitic. It should be either in seventy plus years or never. The moratorium, let's admit, does not offend against justice: it illuminates with a hundred watermarks and a thousand scenes the very beautiful and austere book of the law.

Nobody's Fault but His Majesty's, Sugar

Let's stop groping in the dark undergrowth that the rays of the Enlightenment sun streaming from on high cannot reach. Let's come out in broad daylight. Let's pretend that we have not subjected the praiseworthy scruples of the best to their hairsplitting conclusions. Let's pretend, just between us slaves, that we did not feel the venom of rejection under the honey of mercy. And let's consider, this time, the generosity of the words and the efficacy of the strategy.

As is well known, the Marquis de Condorcet wrote his *Réflexions* under a pseudonym that he chose with the clear intention of placing himself outside of Catholicism and France, and placing himself squarely within the cause of the Negro slaves. He describes himself as Swiss, calls himself Schwartz ("Negro" in German), and declares himself "Pastor of the Holy Gospel in Bienne." But everyone knew from the very first day that the *Réflexions* was by Marie-Jean Antoine Caritat, Marquis de Condorcet. Is he hiding? Rather clumsily, if one goes by the testimony of the period when his book was published and reissued. Does he want to suggest that "Mr. Negro" by sole virtue of this borrowed family name is better suited than "The Marquis" to the complexity of the disaster that he evokes and denounces? I do not know. I observe more readily, however, that the Marquis adopts a lofty attitude and resolutely sides with the French *philosophes* and encyclopedists of the period on a practice that they never abandon. Montesquieu, the patrician of Bordeaux, and a shareholder in a slave-trading company, had set the tone in this matter. He was moved to pity by the excesses of slavery, an institution about whose management and maintenance he was coolly calculating, and yet accused Spain of sucking the lifeblood of America and Africa. And before giving wise counsel to the great and powerful of this world, to everyone, on how best to administer the enslaved Negroes in their colonies, he deigned to dream of a convention that they, the powerful, would all be signatories to out of mercy and pity for those whom destiny had riveted to slavery.[32]

"All the great of this world." What does this mean? Montesquieu also displayed his Frenchness with panache. Wouldn't he have stood a better chance of being more effective by summoning France's great ruler to preach by example? So it seems to me. But it is possible that to the lofty universality of reason only corresponds the fuzzy universalism of the address: no great and powerful person in this world had the least reason to feel particularly targeted by Montesquieu the slaver.[33]

After him, does anything change on this issue, which no one would consider trivializing as mere rhetoric? Let's read on to see. Rousseau, who resolutely condemned classical slavery, did not notice that the slave trade and the ordeal of Negroes in the Caribbean raised a philosophical problem, if only on the palpably empirical level of the inventory of the detrimental effects of technology. Why then should he have thought it useful to address anyone to put an end to anything?[34] Whatever the outrageous remarks, anachronistic for the time, that Voltaire may have made on the diversity of origins of the different human races, he was acerbic in his criticism of those who, on the pretext of their difference, claimed the right to subjugate others on the pretext of their inferiority. But this does not prevent him from lapsing occasionally and making an animal of the slave. And then during his addresses to the powerful against slavery, he too would rather criticize all and sundry in general than Versailles in particular. Diderot and Raynal, whose private income was hardly distinguishable from their supplementary income from slave traders, adopted a similar attitude.[35]

For all of them, the absolute reference was the extermination of the Indians and Spain's settlement "policy" in the archipelagoes and the lands of the setting sun. Spain and Portugal started it, and the other nations of Christendom followed suit. The two peninsular kings were not stopped on their crime trail. Instead, they became the object of jealousy. When Africa was being bled, Portugal and Spain were no longer the only countries involved. But this was before the Enlightenment. Can France be stopped now that the radiant lights of the Enlightenment are shining on her? Forget it. In this glorious eighteenth century, the economic stakes of civilization, the intensity of maritime, commercial, and "industrial" competition were such that each nation saw the unilateral abandonment (as they would put it today) of the system of slavery as leading, without doubt, to the collapse of a pillar of its own national, political, and economic system. No one, physiocrat or not, theoretical defender of free labor or not, pointedly asked Versailles to put an end to the massacre. The request, the demand, was rather addressed to all the great of this world, which is why they could each afford an elegant response that had only been too clearly suggested to them: "I would very much like to, but I doubt that my example will be followed by others, and I'll lose my trade." Perfect.

Universality of reason or not, the specific historical context of each philosophy or not, one would like to find in the calmly colonialist, and only occasionally antislavery, production of the Enlightenment in France a healthy balance in the tone of the addresses and the names of their addressees between moral, political, and philosophical urgency on the one hand, and the concern for efficacy on the other. Universal reason is preachy with everyone and accommodates everyone. Does it really condemn anyone? By chasing after too many goals, you end up achieving none. By depicting the statue of the black Spartacus on a plinth made up of all the crowns and scepters, like Mercier, Raynal, and Diderot did,[36] the great day is indefinitely postponed, and the French crown is never truly asked to do justice to the slaves. Versailles is encouraged to show "mercy and pity." The crown, a dutiful daughter, reduces by a good dozen the maximum number of lashes with which the slave's back will again and again be lacerated—signed Louis, the sixteenth of that name.[37]

With Condorcet, it is hardly any different. Out of concern for efficiency, I imagine, he does not once mention the *Code noir,* that exclusively French document and a pure product of Versailles, which contains the law and rules governing the slave-trading business, a business not "tolerated" but legally elevated to the status of a state institution. He talks of "the Negro islands of America and Africa," of states that "tolerate" the enslavement of Negroes, while France—and several countries in the wake of her bright example—codified it. He looks "all over Europe for a dozen men" that would be indifferent to the attraction of gold and manioc, and monitor, on the spot, (where else?) the implementation of the moratorium, and seems to be satisfied with that, although twelve men to cover all the colonies seems like a lot of work for so few workers! His notes refer to reports and memoirs concerning France or the others. He doles out advice pell-mell to the Spanish and the French on the allocation of "small plantations" to whites. As for the Negro slaves, we all know they do not count and will have to wait several decades. He foresees finally (and we have just spent some time on that) how France would resettle Protestants and Jews and is reassuring about how the Dutch and the English would not fail to act in a similar way. The French, English, and Dutch can do it. Condorcet is convinced about it, and shortly after stating it, he launches out on a colorful, irrefutable diatribe against Spanish clericalism and its crimes, a diatribe whose central argument is that the strong influence of the church on this country makes any hope of opening up its colonies to Protestants and Jews illusory, which to Condorcet is a monumental error. But to my knowledge, the France of Condorcet's day had not repealed Articles 1 and 2 of the *Code noir,* which forbade any other religion or practice in the colonies except that of the Roman, Apostolic, and Catholic Church. So, why then the gratuitous tirade against Spain? Mr. Schwartz is indeed engaged in a dialogue with all of Europe, mindful of this political realism, which, as we saw a moment ago, results in disengagement under the guise of an all-out offensive.

"Men distinguished by their merit, honored with the esteem of the public, and enjoying preeminent positions in the four principal nations of Europe, all own plantations that are cultivated by slaves (. . .). With each passing day that they delay working toward breaking the chains of their slaves [they] stain themselves with a new crime." It is Spain, France, England, and Holland that Condorcet summons and implores all at once to put an end to the infamous traffic, to rethink the "so-called importance of the sugar colonies." But a peremptory, differential, ringing accusation from him against the Crown, which guarantees the perfect legal functioning of this most monstrous of institutions called the *Code noir*? Not a single word, which is what the universality of reason, the global nature of the sugar market, the theoretical and political comfort of Montesquieu's address to "all the great and powerful of this world" can result in.

It is up to each person to admire the Enlightenment unreservedly or to reject its prejudice with no regrets. Let the courage of the encyclopedists be cheered to high heavens, the cowardice of theologians or the strenuous action of the clergy endlessly fustigated. The fact remains, however, that the direct attack on the authorities with ultimate responsibility for slavery—in the name of no consideration other than that of the inviolability of man, as it is taught and proclaimed by philosophy and theology—is the work of Las Casas and, in his wake, of a small handful of Spanish monks.[38] In the way the Enlightenment prosecutes it when it gives thought to it, this struggle for the Negro as a human being (which parallels but falls well short of that of Las Casas for the Indian and the Negro as human beings and as a sovereign people) smacks too much of sugar from beginning to end, from Montesquieu to Condorcet to Grégoire.

For centuries, scholars will continue to argue about the debt of the explosion of Saint-Domingue to the Enlightenment,[39] the depth of rejection of neoscholastic debates by the Enlightenment. It must be constantly acknowledged, however, that while great for whites and from a Euro-Christian and Eurocentric reading of the universe and history, the initiatives of the Enlightenment in matters concerning the enslaved Negro, the emancipatable or freshly emancipated Negro, never rise above the pathetic level of the accounts book where records of shipping and trading transactions in pounds per tonnage or in hundreds of kilos are calculated—a language and attitude that must have been the decisive factor "in the final analysis," as the expression goes, but a language and attitude that in no way influenced the titanic but lonely and doomed struggle of Las Casas, a language and attitude that Toussaint Louverture rejects and erases in order to let bloom, at last, the language of liberty by itself and for itself.

Las Casas speaks to Spain and its king. Louverture speaks to France and its rulers. But French philosophy, when it deigns to talk about Negroes, vilifies everyone in general and no one in particular, something that French historiography is proud of when it creeps into the language of power. It celebrates, in this form of disengagement through tactical excess of engagement, yet another form of its laughable universal philanthropy. Louverture settled the question, not the Enlightenment; Dessalines, not Napoleon.

CHAPTER 2

The Market of Equals

"All French Men Are Born and Remain Free and Equal"

It was in Bamako. Mali was commemorating in its own way the bicentennial of the French Revolution. Not without a touch of rebelliousness. By way of general remarks on the contribution of the French Revolution to Africa, Malians were staging the encounter between France and Africa with a title that needed no commentary: "Blue-White-Black." At the heart of their performance was the memory of a truth—slavery—and of a text—the *Code noir*—which the actors had made central to their contribution to the worldwide glorification of the Enlightenment and its revolutionary outcome. In Bamako, in a hall full to capacity and chokingly hot, an internationally famous lawyer, Mr. Diallo, took the floor and spoke about himself: "I remember that when I was a monkey . . ." The hall burst into laughter and applauded noisily. Mr. Diallo continued his remarks, narrating his memories as a monkey. He was not present during the great period of the triangular trade and therefore could not remember it. He was not present at the time of the Berlin Treaty[1] any more than he was in the days of Jules Ferry, in the era of Jules-Ferryism. No, at the time of the Native Code *(Code de l'indigénat)*,[2] he was a monkey, according to him, and so remained between the end of the Native Code and the day his country became independent.

"I became a human being the day, hour, and minute my country attained sovereignty, the day I became, in my country, a citizen of my country; the day the language of the colonizer ceased to speak on my behalf, to define me."

For Mr. Diallo, Malians in Mali did not emerge from their condition as subhumans with the Enlightenment, with the Revolution, or indeed with the dust clouds of the African cavalcades of the Third Republic—a republic that claimed, though, to have abolished slavery out there. One does not necessarily become a human being the day one gives oneself the instruments of one's destiny, but the moment one can narrate one's memories as a monkey, to weep or laugh about them.

Who then opened floodgates in the riverbed of emancipatory thought? There has been a misunderstanding. Someone opened these gates to divert the flow of its current, and we would like to know who did it! The discourse of the Enlightenment—if not since Montesquieu then at least since Rousseau, and very clearly since Voltaire on the one hand and Diderot on the other—cannot tolerate the denigration or bestialization of man wherever he may be. If the contemporary African searches his memory long enough for the slave and monkey of yesterday, he cannot objectively erase from his recollections the eruption of a universalism, a philanthropy that embraced him within a perfectly homogenous, generic whole.

He does not recall these memories, which means nothing was explained to him. The story told him was narrated in such a way that he cannot recognize himself in it. What the European, his mentor, interprets as the logical outcome of universal philanthropy—the civilizing mission given by history to the nations of Christendom[3]—the Negro sees as the well-ordered succession of different modalities of subjugation and dehumanization, depending on the needs of each period and the technical possibilities of the moment. Strengthened by the conquest of the territory of his memory, the black man, formerly a slave, sees stretching out before him anthropometry consultancies whose sizes correspond to the former raiding and commercial zones of the slave trade at its height.

Tell him that he is wrong. Ask him to change his mind and to put things in perspective. Which perspective, he will ask you? With the best will in the world that he is capable of summoning, he will come out with Galliéni's name where you were expecting Brazza's. But let's say he comes out with Brazza's. Where you expected a passionate couplet on colonization through "evangelical" disinterestedness, you instead get a long-winded speech on the importunate paternalism of a man who exhausted load carriers just as severely as leaders of other caravans of exploration, reconnaissance, and subjugation. There has been a misunderstanding. The Malian lawyer had long been a human being—his ancestors too—but he still thought himself a monkey. He had long been a citizen, but he still thought himself a subject. He was master in his own country, but he still thought himself a slave. He was already everything, yet he believed himself to be nothing. In the final analysis, was this independence to which he attached so many virtues—when in reality it only gave him what he already had—not granted rather than acquired? And why did the clowns in his country resort to the indecency of plastering the color of the *Code noir* on the flag of all the liberties?

Either the descendants of slaves are truly monkeys, or someone—but who, on whose powerful authority—had corrupted the language of the Enlightenment along the way to make it say what the Enlightenment never said.

Back to Bamako: an investigation, a survey conducted with the means available. This was at the height of the bicentennial celebrations, in the context of fervid Francophile passions that were to be displayed by all those who, in the heat of sub-Saharan Africa, collaborated or cooperated (if this word is preferable). The question was asked: does anyone know about the 1789 Declaration? The majority of pupils, high school graduates, and members of the capital's intelligentsia consulted knew the answer. Various combinations and classifications were made. Who knows what Article 1 of the Declaration says? Yes, Article 1 stipulates, according to most of the responses to the survey, that "All French men are born and remain free and equal." It stops there, and that statement in its touching brevity forces us to go back to the sources and to conclude that there has been no falsification of thought, no diversion of the flow of the current of Enlightenment thought. Its core elements have been kept. Were Malians given this sophisticated interpretation of the opening of the Declaration out there in their country? The answer is: clearly not. On their own, in their schools, in the crushing heat of the sun, they had worked out the most precise interpretation possible (when the interpreter is a black man) of Article 1 of the Declaration, the article that governs the entire declaratory and pompously declamatory construction of the Declaration.

The Declaration is often considered the finest jewel of all this formidable intellectual production that we think of when we talk about the Enlightenment. Nobody will question the relevance of the pre- and post-Marxist materialist critiques of the bourgeois and strongly class-centered foundations of the first and subsequent Declarations. Further research will benefit from a study of the work, the preparatory debates, and all the scattered but deeply related elements of which the Declaration is the highest synthesis. It remains true, however, that not enough emphasis has been placed on the fact, when it is even mentioned, that the black slaves appear twice as such in the charter only to be tossed out of the text and coldly excluded from any description of the inalienability and imprescriptibility of their rights.

A close reading of each of the articles cannot suggest in any way whatsoever the slightest wish to exclude the slaves. "Men are born and remain free and equal in rights." Collective memory embellishes what it chooses to embellish. It has modified the first article to read: "All men are born and remain free and equal." It added "all" because it was used to thinking of men in their genericness (a practice derived from "prejudice" dating back to well before the Enlightenment). It eliminated "in rights" because it had in mind, once again, the founding, prefatory will of genericness from which right derives but which right does not found (an idea that the Enlightenment read in the heart of "prejudice," and did not invent). It therefore celebrates in this opening expression, as "amended," the universality and the obvious naturalness of the equality of all. So much the better if memory improves on what it remembers, and better still if what it imposes, although false, enriches the significance of something whose truth it chose to forget.

For the "men" of this first paragraph are born and remain free and equal in rights, but however numerous they may be, they do not constitute the totality of all men. The Negro slaves and the saleable Negroes are (all) not part of that number, unless, of course, those Negroes are not men but movable assets as the *Code noir* specifies. And in that case, certainly, the "men" of Article 1 refers to "all men" because since the slaves are not men, the declarants would have heaped ridicule on themselves by putting "pickaxes" (that is how the colonists called their slaves) in the category of the "free and equal in rights." It is therefore important to read the opening of this first article literally, important not to stretch its meaning beyond the Declaration's intent, a declaration that affirms hard-won gains that the rhetoric of prejudice could also, perhaps, have used to adorn itself.

The meaning of the Declaration is today clear to everyone. It has nothing to do with the disgraceful late-night street dances of July 14, 1989, when France was mothering dwarfs whom it transformed into people through its life-giving breath. The project, magnificent in itself, sought to deliver each man, each woman—each woman—of the Old Regime from their status as "subject" and to grace them with the splendors of citizenship. Legal existence and "subjecthood" were therefore prerequisites for any meaningful and comprehensive claim to "citizenship." The subjects of His Majesty the King of France should no longer be subjected to arbitrary rule but to a legal order deriving from the political force of a body of rights and duties set forth in the form of a "declaration that is constantly present to all the members of the social body" constituting up to then the sum of the king's subjects, falling both within the jurisdiction of the law and the arbitrary rule of Capetian monarchs.

It is impossible to read the Preamble of the Declaration and to pretend, on reflection thereafter, to give to the expression "men" in Article 1 a meaning more extensive than that determined by the social body. Given the stakes involved both for history and for our present purposes, forgive me for reproducing in its entirety, without censorship or embellishment, this rarely quoted preamble:

> The representatives of the French people, constituted as
> a National Assembly, and considering that ignorance,
> neglect, or contempt of the rights of man are the sole causes
> of public misfortunes and governmental corruption, have
> resolved to set forth in a solemn declaration the natural,
> inalienable, and sacred rights of man: so that by being
> constantly present *to all the members of the social body,* this
> declaration may always remind them of their rights and
> duties; so that by being liable at every moment to compari-
> son with the aim of any and all political institutions, the
> acts of the legislative and executive powers may be more
> fully respected; and so that by being founded henceforward

on simple and incontestable principles, the demands of the *citizens* may always tend toward maintaining the Constitution and the general welfare. In consequence, the National Assembly recognizes and declares in the presence and under the auspices of the Supreme Being, the following rights of Man and the *Citizen*.[4]

Thus the French people declared. They wanted this declaration, constantly present to all the members of the social body, to forever remind them of their rights and duties. They wanted the demands of the citizens to always revolve around maintaining the Constitution and the general welfare. Men and citizens, constituted as a social body—that is the *Man* of the Declaration, the *citizen* capable of demanding, the one who is a member of the social body.

Let's assume we knew nothing, absolutely nothing about the tragedy of blacks and the Afro-Caribbean genocide, that history had erased everything about it. What would that matter since we carry on with our lives oblivious of this anyway? With this assumption in mind, let's move on, as collective memory has done, from "men" to "all men," and let's make of Article 1 the quintessence of a movement of thought free of all blemish. But let's read this declaration with the *Code noir* in hand (a *Code* whose existence was no mystery to any of the declarants). No matter how much the declaratory text and the declamation that introduce it are dissected and analyzed, there is no risk that it will yield what its letter denies and its spirit does not affirm. The drafts of the text, where, sometimes, the white color of equals appears, are not the text. The representatives of the French people did not want to think of the slave, because he is not a member of the social body. The French people have nothing to tell him, no right to remind him of. He does not belong to the body that constitutes the citizenship of the citizen, because he never was a member of the group that constituted "the subjectness" of the subject.

He was not a subject. He was the property of the king's subject; he remains the citizen's property. He was nothing then and is nothing now. He is not born, because he is not born to the law: he is a slave. And the frightening situation of his nonexistence does not even frighten, two centuries later, the clerical beatitude of the unconditional praise singers of a grandiose text that tramples him afoot, and crushes him with its heels like mere dust.

Dust? Oh no! Property! Excluded in the preamble, eliminated in Article 1, the enslaved Negro triumphs in Article 2, which reads:

> The purpose of all political association is the preservation
> of the natural and imprescriptible rights of man. These
> rights are liberty, property, security, and resistance to
> oppression.

The black man may perhaps not exist , certainly not in a state of liberty and security or of resistance to oppression. And in any case what is the relationship between slavery and "political association"? And can one be everywhere at the same time? But the Negro sits enthroned in property. He does not possess it. He is property. Ontologically, legally, specifically, exclusively, he is property, only property. Yesterday's social body produced the *Code noir* in order to keep this piece of property outside the category of subject. Today's social body produces a declaration that ties this property, beast of burden, pickaxe, and furniture to its citizen-proprietor. A sense of propriety will restrain, I imagine, the tongue or pen of anyone who at this point would argue against what this preamble and the first two articles say, or leave unsaid, when read alongside the *Code noir,* by pointing to other silences that no one, in good faith, has ever used to tarnish the brilliant wonders of the Declaration. But I know the issue of tax-based citizenship will inevitably be raised at this point, as will, unfailingly, that of women and Jews. Well, let's take it into consideration!

There is no better pretext to put their justification to the test than these supposed but "unavoidable" objections.

The spirit and letter of the Declaration and its preamble will legitimize, with use, a gradation in the exercise of the right to vote and in that of other expressions of the effective neglect of the condition of subject, and of the proclamation of the quality of citizenship. But it will be wise to note that the word "female citizen" appears just when that of "male citizen" crops up. It will be fair to add that the additional coercion of which the Jew is victim in no way attacks his status as a human being, and also necessary to acknowledge that women and Jews—to give only the two inevitable examples of eternal common sense—are, whatever the circumstances, neither dispossessed of their humanity nor of their membership of the social body, because no one dared banish them from the above community of "subjects." That banishment, whose explanation is of an ontological-legal nature, is the major and exclusive privilege of the slaves, of those who should have gone through time without leaving the slightest trace in history other than their presence in the accounts books of their citizen-owners. A sense of decency and restraint dictate that one be careful not to mix things up. Is the universal bread soup preferable? In that case everything is for the best in the best of all worlds, and we can simply forget about the slaves and masturbate intellectually by shedding tears for the sad fate of female citizens subjected to the infamous impulses of male citizens, or for that of Jews of both sexes obliged to carry insignia of safe conduct and rush off to their districts at the sound of vesper bells. Who would have the effrontery to compare the stupidity of men and the ringing of vesper bells to the planter's whip? Who? Everyone, or rather no one!

For everyone prefers to lament the misfortune of the forgotten women and of the barely formal citizenship with which they are graced, to lament that of Jews mortified by the extremely short delay in their accession to citizenship. The radical nature of certain critiques of the "outcasts" of the Revolution is constantly referred to in the historiography of these events either to exaggerate or to minimize the meaning that should be attributed to these acts of neglect. But how about the indifference to the inhumanity suffered by the slaves? When people deign to refer to it at all, they do so in half a line, every once in a long while. For the rest of the time, not a word is uttered about it, the pretext being that it is not the place and the right time. Let's be serious.

With Article 1 clearly avoiding the human beings that are omitted in the preamble, and Article 2 allowing the slave to appear only as the property of someone whose liberty, security, and right to revolt are guaranteed right there in the article, common sense would dictate that the inquiry be stopped immediately, and that the treasure hunt for the great absentee in the law be abandoned. Does one wish to find him in the succeeding articles? Then one must be ready to give the full, appropriate meaning to the distinction made here and there between "man" and "citizen," all the while making sure the Negro realizes he is welcome into a generic humanity only a section of which is covered by citizenship. The natural man (referred to in his generic essence outside the expression "rights of man") appears in Articles 7 and 9, which are devoted to the equality of each person before the praetorian and palatine expression of the law. Is the Negro of the plantations part of this universality? No. In the area of charges, court proceedings, and arrest, the *Code noir,* in full force when the Declaration was proclaimed, prescribes a different law from the law,[5] a different law whose abolition the Declaration does not proclaim because the declarants, though fully aware of its existence, simply chose not to know about it. The preamble and the first two articles impose this restriction and ignorance. We must conclude from this that the "man" of Article 7 is not the slave and acknowledge what we already know: namely, that the slave who is accused, arrested, and detained according to a law different from the law does not figure in the category "man."

The slave does not figure either in the "man" of the expression "Every man is presumed innocent until proven guilty" of Article 9. How could the *Code noir* have foreseen the possible innocence—other than "canonical" and deriving in that case from ecclesiastical matters that the *Code* justifiably does not deal with—of "someone," objectified by his status as property, and whose "guilt" or responsibility is a matter left legally to the caprice of his owner? For the slave for whom it does not care a thing, the Declaration is content to state the commonsense expression that outside the "social body" the slave is nothing but property and cannot therefore be an actor in the theater of laws.

Unless, of course, one decides to subject to rigorous interpretation what could be viewed as the sign of an innocent omission. Let's try. In which case the slave will still find himself in the condition to which the preamble consigned him: outside humanity. The "genericness" referred to in Articles 7 and 9 must be taken literally, with no restrictions or cheating: the slave is sent back to where he was, to the condition of animal that he rightly deserves from the moment he got himself entangled in the slaver's net or docked at the quay of a Caribbean port in his cattle boat. Now this zoomorphism cannot possibly be confused with any of the degrees of legal precariousness affecting such and such a category of men in the community or the aggregate of subjects promoted to citizenship. In this regard, the writings of the members of the "Society of the Friends of Blacks" or Mirabeau's memoir against slavery do not contradict this desire to leave the slave where he is; they confirm it. The horrors of slavery are endlessly debated. But let the need arise to condemn its duration, ridicule its alleged necessity, or summon its abolition, and you will see these men of letters and of the law—great minds and authors of so many imperious expressions—suddenly incapable of finding the appropriate word to strike dead the animal in the slave and to salute the humanity of the Negro. Such a death sentence and outpouring would have propelled the slave to the heart of humanity and citizenship—an act tantamount to the wrecking of the tools of Caribbean economic production indispensable to the well-being of the metropole. No way this could be done. The slave must not cross the threshold of the law.[6] A simple and appropriate reaction to this logical conclusion is silence. One reads Mirabeau, and one moves on.

We were in Article 9. With his eyes on the *Code noir,* the reader rapidly goes through the next articles up to the sixteenth. Nothing in particular arrests his attention given that the display of the positive consequences of the sovereignty of the citizens that constitutes the substance of these articles is so many light years away from the contemporary situation of the French slave in the tropics. The Negro slave has waited long enough. And great good it did him. He emerges triumphant and with panache in Article 17, the last article. Sent to limbo from the first line of the Declaration, he rises to the pinnacle in its final sentence. Finally, they thought of him. Could it be that the declarants did not sufficiently proclaim the charm of property ownership? Didn't they make themselves clear enough? Didn't they sufficiently insist on the seriousness of one of the natural, inalienable, sacred, imprescriptible rights of man—the right to property? This is possible, which is why they clarify things in this Article 17, which crowns the whole:

> Property being an inviolable and sacred right, no one may be deprived of it except when public necessity, certified by law, obviously requires it, and on condition of a just compensation in advance.

Why the emphasis? Why the reference to the general interest over the particular interest? The immediate context is well known. The declarants did not have the peculium of the slaves in mind (a peculium the slaves could not possibly get if one seriously follows Rousseau's very serious logic in examining, the better to deconstruct them, the notions of man, property, slave, allowance),[7] because they were unconcerned about their humanity. Has a mule or hinny ever been seen freeloading in the feeding trough, and hoarding rations of oats? What the declarants had in mind was church property above all. What they were talking about was compensation for these gentlemen of prejudice. Who could possibly hold it against them! Conceived for France, Article 17 was to have a fine career in the sugar islands. It was remembered long after Toussaint Louverture, long after the dogs of De Noailles and Napoleon's expedition,[8] when the debate on the abolition or preservation of slavery was finally initiated. And talk about the inviolability of property? What a godsend! "Abolish, gentlemen, but first reimburse." And springing from the finest organs of French thought were fine-sounding, new, beautiful, and definitive words about the right to a just and prior compensation for the white owner deprived of his Negro livestock. Up to the very end, the slave will remain an animal. He will attain the generic status of "man" only if he is defined as an animal right up to the end, thereby making compensation possible. Does anyone care about his peculium? Dream on. What is of concern is the net loss that his elevation to the nudity of the species would represent for his owner. Let's listen to Schoelcher. Let's listen to Lamartine. Let's listen to Tocqueville. Let's ignore the boastful speeches of the defenders of the idea of the irreducibility of slavery. Their vociferation is of no interest to us. Our concern is with the luminous generosity of those who could no longer stand the fact that there should exist on the fringes of humanity beings whose nature is not suitable for the noble notion of citizenship. Well, they all rediscovered the letter and spirit of Article 17 of the Declaration.

Schoelcher fought unfailingly for the freedom of the slaves from as far back as 1840. Before this date, he gave thought to the idea of a moratorium that should precede abolition. What will be the duration of that moratorium? Forty or sixty years seemed reasonable. But both before and after his proposed moratorium, whether he was in support of a delay in every point similar to the one to which Condorcet was resigned or indeed of immediate abolition, Schoelcher found the pure justice of compensating masters in the higher interest of national trade (masters suddenly deprived of their imprescriptible right to property) indisputable.

Lamartine could not accept the idea of abolition. He was more resigned to the establishment of a moratorium than he actually demanded it, a moratorium during which the slaves would quietly learn to be free, with no loss to their owners.

Two days before the abolition of slavery, Tocqueville became an abolitionist. Before that he panicked at the thought of the destruction of whites by suddenly freed blacks. He refined his judgment and came round to accept abolition but specified: "if slaves have the right to be free, it is indisputable that the colonists have the right not to be ruined by the freedom of slaves."

Three simple examples (cases of the ultimate reduction of the slave to the pure reality of his price) that prove that Rousseau's conclusive analysis, and his point about a fundamental aberration in linking together "slavery" and "rights," was indeed sound. But let's leave Rousseau there; let's even go as far as to forget that in the course of the same analysis the *philosophe* does not breathe a word about the Franco-African slave trade.[9] Let's make only very brief reference to Raynal's equivocations (already him) in settling the conflict between the necessary liberty of slaves someday, the unquestionable French right of possession and exploitation of the islands, and the inalienable property rights of the colonists.

With Schoelcher, Lamartine, and Tocqueville, we are at the period when the slaves would cease to be slaves when these Negroes whom "we nearly mistook for intermediary beings between animal and man" (Tocqueville, again) would come to the end of the process of their humanization. Unless one is deaf or blind, one will see in this rhetoric the ultimate confirmation of what the Declaration foresaw in its last article. Livestock can only become human on condition that the breeder be paid the price per head of cattle that is shortly to leave the barn, a condition that the nation proclaims to be in its interest. It is pointless to claim that there has been malfeasance, perversion of meaning in giving ontological or anthropological significance to measures that are purely commercial. The person who makes such a claim would have to blush almost immediately for tolerating this semantic shift from the ontological to the "mercurial" only when it comes to Negroes. The shift seems intolerable for all other categories of human beings.

Is that what the Enlightenment wanted? It said nothing that clearly opposed this "drift." It did not see the Negro. It therefore kept him out of sight. All it saw in him was the promise of a quantitative progression of the potential, "man." When the Enlightenment went into decline, the romanticism of the leading thinkers that came after it did not know how to shed its bankruptcy. Who would doubt Schoelcher's consistency and courage? But the liberator of the slaves of the French Antilles, the gravedigger of the *Code noir* was also, at the same time, one of the bards of the enslavement of Africans in their homeland, on their soil in Africa, an enslavement that was allegedly painless but enslavement all the same.[10]

When closely examined, there is no doubt about the statement: "All Frenchmen are born and remain free and equal in rights." The Bamako survey led to the most accurate response, historically, to the question asked. The rest? The rest was already the business of Toussaint Louverture and the slaves of Saint-Domingue.

But after these grandiose beginnings for all but nonexistent for the slaves, what else was there? There was one more development whose slow progress through various texts, declarations, constitutions could be followed until November 4, 1848, when the sovereign people, through the voice of its representative bodies, finally recognized in the lapidary concision of Article 6 of the Constitution: "slavery cannot exist on any French territory." Did the Second Republic, which put a final end to the scandalous history of slavery, ever make any reference to the Enlightenment? It is well known that rather than enthusing over the dying embers of an eighteenth century in its twilight, the Second Republic drank its fill of inspiration from the waters of Romanticism. One would clearly have to manipulate (as usual) the history of ideas and of constitutions to establish a direct link between the forgetfulness of 1789, the farce of 1794, the imperial stampede of the beginning of the nineteenth century, and the turn of events in 1848.[11]

Along the way, at the very moment when in Saint-Domingue the slave would breach the walls of history with a cry of immense reverberation, we come across another major text, one of those that fill the common Frenchman who reads them with pride but that restore a new authenticity to the invulnerability of the slave trade, of slavery, and of the Negro's nonhumanity. The text in question is the preamble to the Constitution of September 3, 1791, whose body is stiffened with strong words:

There shall henceforth exist neither nobility, peerage, hereditary distinctions, distinctions by order, feudal regimes, patrimonial justice, nor any of the titles, ranks, and prerogatives deriving from them; neither order of chivalry, guilds, decorations that require proof of nobility or that presuppose distinctions of birth, nor any rank higher than that of public servant in the exercise of his duties. There shall exist neither public office, inherited or bought, nor, for any section of the nation or for any individual, privilege or exception to the common law of all Frenchmen. There shall

exist neither assemblies of jurors nor corporate bodies for
the professions or trades.

September 3. Everyone will notice (perhaps not) in this theory
of peremptory abuses, the absence of the one person whose
unbearably scandalous situation still does not appear in the
thinking of the period. The text states that feudalism is abolished, wonderful. But it does not state that slavery is no more.
Just like the 1789 Declaration, the September 1791 Constitution
opts for the cowardice of silence or, if you will, the arrogance of
lies. No more "exception to the common law of all Frenchmen"
anywhere in the nation and for anyone. It is true that if the
islands of the Antilles are only colonies, the slaves are nobody.
So in the arrogance of its lie, the constitution does tell the truth.
In the cowardice of its silence, it is at one with the thinking of
the nation. In 1791, Saint-Domingue was already writing with
flames and knives what the knights of Lady Equality dared not
write decoratively on their parchments for fear of being unworthy of Lady Property. Is that all? Not quite.

Still to come was this grotesque debate on the most appropriate way to name the slaves, while avoiding pronouncing
this word that to be uttered alone was, on Robespierre's word,
a source of dishonor to the constituents who were regulating
the thing. At the end of that month, with Saint-Domingue in
flames from coast to coast, the overseas assemblies—where
neither monkeys, cattle, nor Negroes sat but only colonists—
were charged with the task of drawing up specific laws for the
"un-free."

Is it finally clear? There, references were constantly made
to the Enlightenment. The indecent sniveling was endless.
But there the Enlightenment failed completely, if it had ever
thought of lifting to full and total humanity the unformed
mass of slaves—humanizable eventually but not then—whose
blood, sweat, and death buoyed the trade "surplus" generated
by the French economy, a surplus that enabled these gentlemen

to be rid of their tyrants. The "un-free." Go through the trouble of comparing this cynical attribute to all the rhetoric that from a theoretical angle culminated in the Declaration of the Rights of Man and the Citizen, and which from the practical action that resulted from it led to Napoleon's normalizing enterprise. It is a case of the lions entrusting to the foxes the job of laying down the law in the henhouse, and to the ferrets the law in the hutches.

It would be an open and shut case if this story were read from the vantage point of the slave. What a waste of time on the other hand if one does not care a Republican thing about her and one only dreams of strengthening the white order in its historical, inalienable, and undeniable superiority. Each person in this world makes his choice the way he deems fit and to the best of his ability.

In Bamako, Mr. Diallo was right to count on the amused complicity of his audience. "When I was a monkey . . ." The Enlightenment was incapable of letting his ancestors know that it had long considered them human. This is because it was far from convinced about it. Did it suspect they were? Perhaps.

A Young Black Child in the Boudoir

It happened in the Sorbonne five or six years ago. I was inflicting on the students who were masochistic enough to take my course a reading of Montesquieu's constant compromises with Franco-Antillean slavery. I scrupulously kept to the texts of the patrician of Bordeaux. Faithful to my bad faith and to my choice to interpret the history of ideas and the law from the point of view of the barefooted, the starving, and the slaves, I was not interested—because others examine it well, and rightly so—in the marvels of the separation of powers, whose transcendent importance in the history of ideas and institutions is well known. I spent time instead showing the ease with which one could catch in the same man, at the same time, and in the same texts, so much generosity of spirit in weaving into reason the politics of the privileged, and so much moneygrubbing insolence in justifying, for the France of his time, the continuation of the practice of Roman-like slavery. After a number of sessions and the identification and analysis of Montesquieu's pro-slavery texts,[12] I announced that I would undertake in the following week an examination of Rousseau's pro-slavery proclivities. That was too much for some students. From the middle of the amphitheater a voice rang out: "Montesquieu, very well. But Rousseau, you'll never succeed!" I must confess that in a quarter century of teaching at the Sorbonne, I had never been confronted with such a short, frank, definitive, and terse response.

And yet, in my edition, following others', of the *Code noir* I have demonstrated at length Rousseau's capacity to miss entirely the point of the slave trade and the scandal of slavery in spite of the definitive passage where he condemns the four possible forms of slavery examined by Grotius. I challenge anyone to find and show me the smallest little line where Rousseau condemns the kidnapping of Africans and their enslavement in the Antilles. It does not exist.

And that is understandable. At the dawn of the Enlightenment and during its high noon, Montesquieu, Rousseau, and others did not have a word to say against intra-European slavery, which was also based on a slave-trading, an exclusively slave-trading, economy.[13] Slavery had been practiced earlier, but that was elsewhere. Here and now, the question of slavery got embroiled, from the economic-legal point of view, with that of serfdom. At the political-legal level, the question encompassed the theme of the transcendence of subjection or subjecthood through accession to citizenship. It is therefore important not to lose sight of this strategy of double meaning. It is applicable to the chains that Rousseau saw on the feet of all men and that had to be broken and not loved as it is to Robespierre's tirades on the need to abolish slavery. I systematically ignore the eulogists of the virtues of slavery and pay attention only to "progressive" thinkers: those who quietly rationalize slavery or remain silent about it, those who condemn the manner of its practice but not its principle, or who condemn its principle while deploring, with tear-filled eyes, the fact that it cannot reasonably and rationally be done away with instantly.

In this circle of thought, the parallel is not established between the serf here and the slave there, between the subject here and the animal in the islands. The parallel is drawn over and over again between the subject suffering under the countless rigors of feudalism here in France and the Greek and Roman slave carrying the burden of the empire and the city and kept outside the law in a zone bordering legality. The strategy merely compares comparables. It does not deviate toward the juxtaposition of what could be considered fundamentally different. Now, as we are well aware, neither the whiffs of an intra-European slavery on the decline nor the "strangeness" ("uniqueness" in Rousseau's words) of Negroes constitute data suitable enough for a comparison between the lived state of subjection of the subject and the desired one of sovereignty of the citizen. The reasoning that constantly underpins the emancipatory language of the Enlightenment valorizes the extension of universalism to the directly perceptible uniformity of distinct cultural reference points, and the elevation of all indisputably accomplished humanity to sovereign capacity. The Greek or Roman slave can serve as a term of comparison, and reference is frequently made to him. So can the European serf. The "residual" intra-European slave is ignored, in the strong sense of the term. He is not seen. Neither the holds of galley ships nor the cloisters of Valladolid are examined. The Negro slave, the Negro, naturally a slave, does not fit the criteria of the comparable either on the grounds of universalism, as it is defined, or of accomplishment as it is perceived. The question asked is not "Who is the Negro?" It is most often framed differently as "What is the Negro?" It is in light of this categorization that from Montesquieu to Raynal through to Rousseau, Voltaire, Diderot, Helvétius, and Condorcet, the Negro slave can only approach the precincts of the law stripped of all humanity, draped in his strangeness, or reduced to something trivial through endless moratoriums. Is it exclusively that? I do not know. But the erudite scholar of goodwill must concede to the history of the Enlightenment what the Enlightenment imposes on history. When the Enlightenment says "humanity," it means neither what we mean when we use that word, nor what prejudice means by it.

I do not know, neither do I know if I can know, whether the notion of "humanity" is a creation of Western culture. All things considered, I would rather take a risk with Feuerbach and say that it is a creation of Christianity,[14] not necessarily Western Christianity. It is the liturgy of the Slavic and Byzantine peoples that repeats obsessively and ad nauseam "*Christos, tcheloviekolioubchek* (meaning "Christ, lover of men"). It does not take much to show that the cultures that we use as reference points openly flirt—when it comes to specifying the legal, moral, political, and physiological parameters of man and judging the appropriateness of each and everyone of these inevitably plural profiles—with the standard that is discursively at our disposal, and in whose specular reflection we recognize ourselves as members of the family. From the legal point of view, criteria ensuring the pyramidal distribution of humanity are never lacking. They are developed in light of the meaning of the term sovereignty. But the notion of humanity still remains. Whether or not it is the object of special, preliminary attention is another matter. Yet the distribution of humanity into varieties of humanity is done neither under the rubric of physiology, nor of anthropometrics, nor even of ethics, since each philosophy concedes to each section of humanity the possibility of "doing wrong" or, in the language of canon doctrine,[15] of "being unmeritorious." The criteria by which one is admitted to or excluded from the category "man" are expressed first and foremost in the language of the law. Of course, the law, or any premise of normativity, is the developed form of recognition or rejection, a form preceded by others. That notwithstanding, the translation of exclusion and inclusion into positivity—whatever the dimension that one wishes to give to this term—is an indication of the effectiveness of the operation of selection that results in recognition or rejection. If I choose to read these stories from the vantage point of the excluded, it will be understandable that I have to highlight their narration right where it first appears and where it undeniably matters, namely, in the area of legal and, in any case, normative criteria. They can be justified afterwards by any set of arguments.

This is how it is for strangers. This is also how it is for slaves. For pagans, it is quite different. For Negroes, it is completely different. To argue that the Greeks had no notion of humanity, man, or the subject is an interesting philosophy exercise. Foucault wrote some remarkable passages some years ago on the invention of man.[16] Dialectical materialism has examined with exemplary steadfastness the theme of man-in-project, a theme whose beginnings, without even probing the question further, can easily be traced to Kant but also to Auguste Comte, who approached it differently. But the Greeks, who are sometimes gracefully thought to have been uninterested either in the humanity of man or the specificity of the subject—preoccupied as they were with regulating the life of the *polis* both in its everyday and exceptional aspects—would be surprised to learn that they are perceived to have reduced humanity to beehives or anthills on the subject of work or feasting, or to processions of pilgrims in search of incantations, miracles, and heavenly gifts on that of sentiment. The "treatise on passions," which they could have written and which can easily be developed from their literary and philosophical production, demonstrates un-ambiguously (and from where would such ambiguity come, had it even been present?) that they knew quite correctly how to pose the problem of man's humanity and of the subject's specificity. The definition changes, and the parameters become more diversified when the question of infusing the human into the social, the fateful into the political, and the specific into the legal arises. Even Aristotle, the man who through beautiful circular thought subordinates the exercise of rationality to that of legality, and legal normativity to the sacredness and correctness of the laws discovered by reason, does not contradict this fact in his reflections on the souls of slaves.[17] In this respect, there is neither a quarantining of the "phenomenology" of humanity nor an alternating process of bestialization and humanization among the neighbors that would take place according to the rhythm of aggressions or alliances. The Trojans were neither hyenas nor calves. They were human beings. Helen does not go to bed with a stallion on a pile of forage but with Paris on a royal bed. You want us to discuss what is elegantly referred to as the absence in these lost civilizations of a doctrine of individual destiny that is said to have flowered only in the Renaissance? Let's do. But in so doing, we will still have to erase from the history of literature all indications of the thousand and one ways in which the Greeks triumph over various forms of destiny and of the equally numerous ways in which medieval man cheats with God and the devil. Everywhere—from the rigors of Plato's *Laws* to Plotinius's rapturous delights, from the soliloquies of the Stoics to Montaigne's reveries—one thing is obvious: the discussion is about humanity, about men, about man. He is placed where he places himself, namely, in a specular relationship with what on his own he sublimates or deifies, but without having to resort to the paralogism of avoiding what he defines as particularly suitable for him. That it was necessary to wait for Renaissance man for it to be possible to speak of man in a manner that is fully consistent with his feelings seems quite natural, not at all extraordinary. To read our classics along the lines of the exclusion or dehumanization of neighbors through successive acts of disengagement from the modalities of the essence by which one achieves kinship is not difficult. The opposite reading is not difficult either. It should be quite easy to present the synoptic table of a *philosophia perennis* with a double entry: continually rejecting the foreignness of the foreigner across centuries and civilizations, and continually extending the definition of man and humanity across centuries and civilizations to the confines of the inhabited world—a world obviously inhabited by men in perpetual conflict among themselves and with their passions.

Anthropologically, the matter seems clear to me: the foreigner is a human being; the slave is a human being; the foreigner's child and the slave's child are born humans.

The matter becomes more fundamentally complicated as soon as we move from anthropology and from a "treatise on passions" to the law. Not that this should be taken to mean a special leap from the stuttering of the soliloquy to the clamor of the courtroom. More modestly but also more radically, it is that anthropology's beautiful harmony becomes grating cacophony as soon as the question arises of translating each person's universalist rhetoric—for Ulysses, Ithaca is the measure of all things—into a calculated distribution of humanity, when, to put it clearly, one moves from passions to legalities.

One is passionately asked to make the shift with all the consequences this entails. The kiss of the law is as cold as the kiss of death and as transcendental as the kiss of love. It creates and destroys you; it transports and transforms you completely. You have for a long time ceased to be the subject of a "universal phenomenology" that has been a-temporal since Cro-Magnon. Your nature, passions, and identity are no longer reiterations that are analyzable with reference to the unity of the model. They can instead be estimated according to a slimy casuistry of rights and obligations. The law accomplishes this double feat of both defining you and distinguishing you. It both posits you and opposes you. You exist because it so proclaims. Because you cannot distinguish yourself from Mr. So-and-So without offence, you are like him, but because you cannot become one with him without disgrace, you are not him.

One essential merit of the philosophy of the Enlightenment is the bare-knuckled war it wages against the "institutions of the law." If one were to reduce the passion of the Enlightenment to a single struggle, it would have to be its struggle against the "legal" naturalness of inequalities, against this ancient "law" of the Old Regime, which drapes itself with a "liberty" that has been quietly instituted in the heart of institutions that perfectly accommodate the will of tyrants and all manner and types of tyranny, a "liberty" that takes its full "meaning," in the favorite words of the Enlightenment, in those processions of men in ermine.

If it was tactless to pick a quarrel with the Enlightenment on the grounds of its inability to protect itself, prophetically, from certain Marxist critiques and a certain Hegelianism castigating its inability to move from concept to the passion of the subject, from generic man to the individual of flesh and blood, it would be appropriate to give its due to the Enlightenment exactly where it allegedly sinned. Right and the law—usually rhetorically distinguished but fundamentally one and the same under the rubric of the norm—can only be formulated in generic terms. They both base their claim on the generic. The generic is also appropriate for philosophy as long as it does not insinuate itself—and even then—in the tortuous recesses of hearts and loins. The Enlightenment gave rise, whether it admits it or not—it does admit it—to a revival in legal thought. The greatest Voltaire is the Voltaire of the Calas affair, the

greatest Rousseau, that of the *Social Contract*. On the opposite side, Herder's grandeur resides in his ability to point out
the failures and nonegalitarian strategies of this legal revival.[18] From the *Spirit of the Laws* to the *Philosophy of Right*,[19]
through the dizzying heights of Kant's imperatives—terribly
Christly, incidentally, except for the breath of the anthropology to which they make reference—the Enlightenment illuminates from dawn to dusk the sky of concepts with a new way
of thinking about the law.

Is this refocusing of all reflection and practice on this field
of man's spiritual activity an acceptable interpretation? If
so, it must then be conceded that the generic befits the Enlightenment. The Enlightenment defines the species and its
behavior in the courtroom and before nature or divinity:
upright, alone in the harmoniously "polished" radiance of its
perfection. Should I perhaps say, the "aligned" radiance of
its perfection? I will restrain myself.

This curious unity, this harmonious whole, functions mar-
velously well. But of what use are they to the little black child
who in the boudoir caresses Madam infinitely better than the
pup with the softest coat? Where does the little boy—whose
senses and sexuality she awakens, and whom she exalts and
smothers in the perfumed heaviness of the air of her boudoir—
fall within the species? Who is the little black boy, if he is at
all?[20] Is he also part of the species? Does Kant include him in
the universality of this imperative that Jankélévitch qualified
as "a categorical prohibitive"?

For no place is made for him in literature. When he happens to appear in engravings and paintings or on furniture,
holding a candle or offering fruits, he is invisible. One turns
on the lights and helps oneself. Legally and generically he is
absent; as a human being, he is nonexistent. Rousseau sent
scientists to "Africa" to investigate and settle once and for all
the issue of the humanity of blacks and the conclusive ani-
malness of monkeys. He had no doubt the scientists would

settle the matter and was convinced that they would do so in the right manner: by placing the black on this side of the limit of humanity, and the monkey beyond the same limit.[21] Was no little black child present in the smart company kept by that loner? It is difficult to believe, but Rousseau did not care two hoots about enslaved blacks. As for Montesquieu, a shareholder in a slaving company, he spelled out in various places in his correspondence the important relationship between Bordeaux's trade—also his—and the slave trade, and the simple need to promote the city's economic expansion through this means.[22] Little black children could also be found in Bordeaux's best boudoirs. Montesquieu did not see them: they were not introduced to him. And who can guarantee that his Lordship did not himself have two or three at his service?

We know from Marcel Koufinkana's unpublished dissertation "Esclaves et esclavage dans la France d'Ancien Régime, 1660–1794" (Slaves and Slavery in the France of the Old Regime, 1660–1794) that there were numerous blacks in Bordeaux. We know that their masters hired them out on duties of hard labor. What could have prevented some of them from helping his Lordship during the grape harvest? For goodness sake! This hypothesis is not useful to me any more than its opposite. But that it can be formulated without any contradiction either in terms or in relation to the contents of Montesquieu's purse, and without radical improbability, is precisely what brings me back to my earlier question: where is the species, where is the unity, or the generic unity of man, if the little black child does not belong to it? And let us be spared at this point the old tune about the precariousness of the existence of the child in the anthropology of those blessed times.[23] No legal or ethical neglect can justify the shift, inadvertent or deliberate, from the concept of child to that of dog or "suckling calf." No legal requirement stipulates that the young black child should be taken for what he obviously is—the child of a human being. And the *Code noir* decrees that he be recognized for what he is (not by the law, which ignores him, but by the master): namely, an animal, a thing, and a slave. Legally he is nothing because the law accounts for him only to strip him in the process of such consideration of all meaningful presence. The little black child who holds the candelabrum is the candelabrum. The little black child who holds the basket is a basket. The one who caresses Madam is a brush, a sponge—I will go no further. The generic essence of man is never stretched to the point of including in its general ambit the trinkets men wear to tend to their appearances, the tools they use to multiply and diversify the activities of their arms or mouths. When the little black child is in the boudoir with Madam, Madam is alone in the boudoir.

Excuse me, but did I hear you say that today's jurisprudence may also have problems making laws for Martians or establishing driving rules for UFOS? So what? We are not going to lump everything together to give ourselves the comfort of an alibi. Let's get back to serious things. Everything that had been written about the universality of philanthropy while the black child was bustling about, the conclusions of the most beautiful speeches made in salons while he played with the dog, were little more than mindless logorrhea, mindless chatter in the face of this situation of absolute denigration. Here, strangeness had been decreed. The decree was carefully dusted and updated: it could not possibly be forgotten. Keeping pets in respectable homes was a trendy practice in eighteenth-century France and elsewhere in our "climes." "In our climes," Montesquieu ecstatically exclaims, Christianity reestablished the age of Numa, which witnessed the disappearance of the master-slave distinction.[24] Christianity did not for all that put an end in our climes to the practice by which children were expected to lick what animals perhaps only lapped up reluctantly. The possible adequacy of today's law to tomorrow's forms of strangeness, an adequacy that is predictable, desirable, and probably realizable after some unfortunate attempts, cannot serve here as a term of comparison but only as a criterion of condemnation. Through a symbology in which on the upper end the law constitutes the motivation, and on the lower end the privileged site of expression, French eighteenth-century thought accommodated itself with a generic essence that condemned the young black child to a state of pure nonexistence because it rejected the evidence of the obvious humanity of the Negro slave, the enslaved Negro.

When Fontenelle compared the monkey with the little black child, the wisdom of one and the idiocy of the other, and concluded with the admission made by the black child that he had learned what little that he knew from the monkey, we finally and conclusively got the picture.[25] The Enlightenment will change nothing substantive to that type of thinking, hardly anything to its form. A language similar both to Fontenelle's,[26] and to the one used much later by our positivist and Christian nations during the period of the final subjugation of Africans in Africa right in the middle of the nineteenth century, could be found amusing during the Enlightenment.

The senseless meaning of the black child's caresses should not be trivialized by invoking, as is always done, the question of the gap between today's moral demands and the easygoing attitude of the people of that period. For there are examples of people of that period who were ahead of the Enlightenment and, as a cautionary measure, had been condemning for a long time the Enlightenment's temporizing by betting unambiguously on the absence of any possible ambiguity on the issue of a human being's membership or nonmembership in the legal category of the human.

Theologians—broodingly somber people (them again)—tossed all casuistry overboard and without even a second thought firmly placed the young black child in the uniform horizontality of the species. Take the example of Claver and a few others. True, they may not be everyone. But one example is enough, once again, to show up these gentlemen of the Enlightenment and of commerce—they are after all the one and the same people—trailing behind by some centuries what ought to have been thought about the unity of the species, which obliges Madam to air her boudoir, free her little black child, and offer herself a pet or sex toy instead.

The bad faith of my analysis cannot get better along the way. All I need (and I have no less a man on my side than the Abbé Grégoire at his best)[27] is to find in a tradition preceding the Enlightenment not only the theory of the full and total humanity of the black child but also a political practice that makes this being unexceptional in the anthropological literature of the day, and I would have "saved," on this score, the thinking that informed the practice, notwithstanding the disaster that this thinking authorized, justified, undertook, and blessed. All alone, Las Casas saved Christianity. All alone, Claver in his passions and blunders did as much.[28] On the other hand a dozen or so great Enlightenment thinkers (I do not have that many to write about)—demanding from the authorities concerned the destruction of the *Code noir*—would not suffice to "save" the Enlightenment from its pathetic collapse into the abyss of genocide. And this shameless rejection of all rational neutrality happened for one simple reason.

All Las Casas had to do, as Grégoire accurately observed, was to refer scrupulously to his theological doctrines to be able to proclaim as soon as it became necessary, two centuries before the French moment, that the black child had nothing to do in Madam's boudoir and that Madam was not alone in it when she was there with him. These gentlemen of the Enlightenment must have endlessly shilly-shallied with their own legal and ideological constructions—of a perfect solidity designed to shore up white domination—to convince themselves and others unreservedly, and with no remorse, that the little black child was no sex toy. The obviousness of Las Casas's statement was,[29] for the Enlightenment, only the thirty-sixth corollary of an argument whose logical development only the cleverest could follow without getting lost along the way, and winding up . . . with some conclusion about the complete stupidity of Negroes.

If the Enlightenment failed where theologians impose the language of today in speaking like Jesus did about the Canaanite (see next chapter), it is precisely because it sacrificed the mystery of the human, as it was called in the past, to a concern with transparence and scientificity. That the word, or concept, *mystery* is philosophically out of place there and sounds like a pretext for the Enlightenment is something I accept. But it will perhaps be acknowledged that the dismantling of the species results in this context in the theoretical justification of this idea of "perfectibility," whose strange and dangerous consequences we have seen and will continue to see.[30]

The young Negro in Nantes, Bordeaux, or Paris finds himself in legal fantasy land, in a tragic situation, if one decides to stick to the character and his period: anthropologically human because he is a child, legally "a movable asset" because a slave, he falls within the law only in relation to the *Code noir,* which legitimates his legal nonexistence and his profound anthropological destitution. This is how the serious thinking of the period, of the Enlightenment, wanted it. And that is how it was, if not wished, at least tolerated by all, from Montesquieu to Condorcet. *The Code noir* stuck to the period, to the little black boy, and to the Enlightenment.

At this stage, I, who in all frankness and bad faith have chosen to put myself on the side of the Negro slave, am not crowing. I will turn the lights off and leave these gentlemen to their moratoriums. Or I will set out for there, the Caribbean, to revisit a good model breeding farm of young black children so that my eyes can come to the rescue of my memory, so that everything will be reported, so that I can find a good example of the sweetness of the language of the best, in order to catch with Condorcet—in the farms of Catholics, Protestants, Jews, where each twilight brings a mixture of the refreshing music of reed pipes and the reddish glow of the sky—the dazzling light of blanco-biblical and blanco-French genius subtly combining in a single act of philanthropy, the "humanization" of the monkey and the "perfectibilization" of the Negro on the naked body of the slave, riveted to the tragedy of his destiny. I leave once again, dear Condorcet, to catch under the heavy eyelids of the Negro, emancipated yet still destitute, the blurry brilliance of his glorious nothingness.

Dawn, after the Night of Prejudice

Was it at the end of the fourth or the beginning of the fifth century? One day, Saint Augustine, the man who knew everything, was asked his thoughts about the wonders and monstrosities described in the narratives of Pliny the Young or the tirades of merchants, and about the strange beings who inhabit the shores where Ulysses and his companions in adversity were shipwrecked: haphazardly, tales of headless men with faces stuck right in the middle of their chest, of others with doglike heads, and of others still with syringe-shaped noses, feeding on perfumes. Then there are the grossly disproportioned one-legged ones who shade their head from the fierce siesta sun with an oversized foot.

Saint Augustine opined. Prejudice told him the right answer, [31] which he wrote down in the *City of God*.[32] "Rubbish in all likelihood. I ask to see, but fear that there is nothing to see. But if they truly exist, why should that bother me? Their shape and color matter not. They think; they are therefore human beings like you and me, because in them like in you and me, reason is the image of God. They are suitable for baptism, charity, and salvation. But in the same breath, I was also told about the 'antipodes.' May I be allowed to express my sincerest doubts about their existence? No one has ever seen these antipodeans, identical to us in every way and supposedly living under the planet, walking with their heads down and their feet in the exact opposite direction to ours. I fail to understand why the human family would have pushed its pilgrimage on earth to that point—or why some of its children would have chosen such an unlikely and uncomfortable home. No, I really do not believe in the idea of the antipodes."

Well before the Berber drew wisdom from prejudice, a Canaanite woman had come up to a Galilean priest to ask him for alms. The Galilean was sarcastic: "It is not right to take the food of the children and throw it to the dogs." "No," replied the woman. "For even the dogs eat the scraps that fall from the table of their masters." The Galilean responded: "O woman, great is your faith! Let it be done for you as you wish."[33] And he invited her to feast with the children at the Lord's Table. The Galilean shattered with a single word the hatred of Jews for Canaanites, of the privileged for the poor, of men for dogs. He asked the dog to table. Prejudice does not abhor excess in the ridiculous.

Between the Berber and the Galilean, another born and bred Jew dared to speak of a law higher than the law, a law so "egalitarian" that it does not care about any membership of a nation, a country, a sex, of anything that makes it possible to classify, establish hierarchies, exclude or banish. Classifications and categories, hierarchies and forms of exclusion will, of course, reappear in his language. It would, however, have been written some centuries before the Enlightenment that it was possible to think in terms of horizontality of rights and obligations for all humankind.[34]

Let's fast forward: Should the long work of the Middle Ages be reduced to the quodlibetic or, if you will, "disputatious" literature that expressed the exhaustion of that age, or to the casuistry that described its rot? We all know it should not. And we all know that between anathemas and persecutions, slaughters and stakes, the Middle Ages established or rediscovered the autonomy of the political, the rational, the subject, and the theoretical model of sovereignty—of divine origin no doubt—whose custodian was, in the final analysis, the people.[35]

What are we to make of Luther—to stick to our neighborhood—and of the formidable upheaval of his Reformation, which shook crowns, nations, tiaras, miters, minds, and hearts? Are we going to attribute that too to dark prejudice? It might be somewhat delicate, shocking perhaps, to attribute to the age of darkness the ennoblement of the subject—in reality the work of the Reformation—or the routing, accomplished by the Reformation long before Descartes and Voltaire, of a certain type of authority, to talk like Tocqueville.

But it is fair, right, logical, and necessary to keep in mind all these types of "progress," knowing that the demands of historical truth would be mocked by anyone who did not place in context the examination of the breakthroughs of so many beautiful lucky finds in the practice of everyday life. The lights of the Enlightenment undoubtedly tormented the darkness of prejudice. But prejudice, tenacious as ever, always swallowed up in the gaping hole of its nothingness the iridescences of the truth that cracked through its darkness, when it did not hurl into the fires of the stakes all those who dared trouble the peace of the dark night.

Is this too schematic a reading, perhaps? No one is asking anyone to reduce such a long pilgrimage of the mind to so little! The Enlightenment, however, committed the error of describing an ages-old effort of reason—a reason that it came to free from the grip of dogmatism[36]—as a profound lethargy of the mind. And yet, the Enlightenment pursued this task with such energy and generosity that it managed to deepen the difference to the point of no longer contrasting reason with reason, authority with authority, analogy with analogy, but rather dogmatism with dogmatism. When one gets to that point, in philosophy as well as in politics, the conflict no longer makes any sense: one rejects outright, not because one has a proposition to advance and defend, but rather a set of truths to impose.

Can you imagine Descartes, Leibniz, and Spinoza—whose high standards of rigor still delight today's reader after frightening yesterday's theological "establishment"—discarding the results of their thinking on prejudice and the conceptual tools that made prejudice understandable, and much more besides it? Had they played that game, it would have been impossible for them to be understood and to bring to the side of reason those backward worlds on which prejudice feeds. Did they or didn't they realize, all three of them—and the question is worth posing to other great minds—that while finding a way around unacceptable prejudice they had to be careful not to reject its logical simulacra and erase the boundaries of its geography? Theologians all three, they realized it,[37] but all three they were conscious of being able to conquer for reason spaces that had been traditionally reserved for the caprices of Olympus, for the thunderous sounds of Sinai, the dazzling lights of Tabor. Theirs, for our purposes, was not a "useless and pointless"[38] struggle against the ghost of prejudice but a harsh confrontation with what was unacceptable at its core, and constituted its quintessence, namely the rapt and trembling submission of reason to dogma. To which they held up the silent respect of reason in the face of the mysteries of its own beginning.

Of course, this respect was the most shocking of heresies for the theologians who know from privilege that there are no more mysteries in the beginning than there are Greek calends in the end. As theologians, the professionals of lies heckled those who subverted, from within, their own language, a language that still remained, even after its subversion, pretty theological. And as theologians, they fought, wielding fierce anathemas, against the brazenness of reason, in the name of dogma. Later, much later, these same professionals must have clearly understood, and made their understanding known, that the "heretics" were connected not to the torrent of lies but to the gentle stream of a rationality that did not have a scrap of the theological in it, and which was lazing on the surface of all this reversal. And in turn, they tried to lie, narrating their "truths" in a language renewed, but not invented, by the "heretics." Should one conclude that all the swashbuckling was only for public consumption? Let's consider the well-known episodes: Spinoza's disappointments,[39] Descartes's European travels.[40] The compromise, if compromise there was, resided in the use of the same grammar, of a similar syntax, to express both a discourse of religion and a discourse of rationality, and in the convergences between the disturbing certainties expressed by one, right from its exordium, and the serenity of the deductions articulated by the other at the end of its peroration.

For the rest, and the rest was everything, philosophy fought against prejudice with a passion that we all know well, with the shortcomings that we have also all known and that contemporary criticism piously continues to list down among the stratagems hatched out by various people to protect streams of "heresies" from the greed of the "inquisitorial" police.

So we would have covered, year in year out, the period stretching from Descartes to Montesquieu, or, if you will, from Occam to Rousseau, with, of course, a brief pause on the works of Descartes and obviously none on Spanish neoscholasticism.[41] So with the suddenness of great things, of the type that disrupt everything, we would have left behind the world of compromise and suddenly taken our place at the bottom of the grand staircase of the palace of knowledge, all ready for the glorious ascent to the throne of reason, of a reason finally accessible to all in all its glory, a reason whose brilliance would forever dissipate the darkness of prejudice. We gave ourselves everything on the one and only condition that we dispossessed ourselves of everything through a kind of cultural contract that is the epigraph to a social contract of similar promise and demand, on the one and only condition that we truly accepted, this time, to change direction and grammar, history and destiny.

History and destiny: it is curious how the juxtaposition of these two words here reminds me as much of the Saint Augustine of the *City of God* as of the Rousseau of *Confessions*.

I place myself—haven't I sufficiently said this?—with perfect bad faith on the side of the slave when these two words, history and destiny, resonate across the centuries out there (I only have a right to duration since I am not even aware of time). Of what use is this dispossession to me, and this reputation that is celebrated within a human community from which I am absent, for the benefit of a humanity to which I do not belong? And for a start, why am I meddling, I who have nothing and therefore am nothing? I am therefore not asked but constrained to listen, from my cattle truck cast outside humanity, to my buyers and sellers making drastic decisions—as they perhaps sip a good cup of coffee with nice sweet sugar in it—that cut into the very flesh of my timeless time, of my being without existence, ordered to watch the upheaval of upheavals, humanity crossing thresholds, the sun of reason rising, and virtue radiating with brilliance, without anyone worrying about my suffering, my resentment, my hatred.

My suffering, by the way, is not doleful since they know I am incapable of emotion; they could not be bothered by my resentment, since they know I am incapable of coloring my memory with regrets. My hatred? The word is inappropriate in my case: wickedness, which, innocently, is more fitting for animals, is appropriate for me and not the noble sentiment that agitates them when they grunt.

After the long night of prejudice, dawn was just that: the sudden appearance of another history, another destiny that men were asked to accept, to accept while struggling hard to break free from all that kept them chained to the past with its interpretation of the law, of authority, and of property, to break free in order to give birth to a new interpretation of the

law, of authority, and of property—an interpretation, however, that leaves me as much a slave as it found me, as much
subhuman as in the past, and as much shackled to the chains
of those who with the help of the Enlightenment were breaking theirs, as indigent under Montesquieu and Rousseau as
I was under the doctors of theology of the Sorbonne, days
that Montesquieu and Rousseau wanted to think had gone
forever.

And yet the rise of the sun of reason had to be ensured,
a sun that, it was known, would reach its zenith and there
stand still forever by improving upon Joshua's achievement
through its own movement, and not just end its row with the
night with a flourish, Joshua who in his modesty knew that
sunset inexorably followed twilight. It was also necessary to
articulate the new law, the new authority, and the new property at this level. Reason was therefore consulted not with
rash boldness as in the past but with the impulsive noncha-
lance of one who invents and does not fear that old fogies will
hold him to account.

One was especially careful not to say that one had failed to
invent the connection between natural right and some sovereign good. One deduced from it with the most natural rigor a
welcome reinterpretation of authority, one of whose basic and
philosophically relevant merits was to safeguard property. In
the course of the interpretation of property in this period, the
problem of slavery and the slave trade, of the trade in and enslavement of Negroes, stood out starkly, a problem that fit in
beautifully with the distribution of land and the apportion-
ment of teaspoons according to the goodwill of the testators,
a goodwill that was smoothly regulated by law in the fashionable world of Christian Blanco-land.

No matter the accusations against prejudice, it heavily influenced a mode of thinking—for better or for worse—that
did not distance itself at all from what prejudice was capable
of saying both about natural law and its three epigones: right,

authority, and property. The grandiose breaks are to be sought in the area of means and ends. And it is more than extra-ordinary that they can be located there, and there! But what if the Enlightenment then—and its readers today—had the necessary seriousness to acknowledge that though brilliant against the enemy, it deliberately helped itself to the latter's arsenal, disarming him against all odds and reducing him to its mercy? If it acknowledged that, would it lose a little or a lot of its brilliance? It would lose it all, because of the claim made right at the beginning: "Before, you were told that . . . Now we tell you this." The perfectly Christ-like ring of the expression does not suit the slanderers of theology, resolutely theologian themselves but unscrupulous theologians. So, let's hear nothing more of that old trick about new wine in old skins that stink of stale glue and goat hair two miles away. The wine should be new, as should the skins. Otherwise, the new gush would be nothing but a steady flow of what had already been drunk, with perhaps the lighthearted fury of a season of abundant harvest. And it would be difficult not to notice, on the pavement in Jena, Balaam's donkey trotting along with the prophet, in the shadow of the thoroughbred horse bridled by the "soul of the world" in braggart's outfit, under the fond gaze of the philosopher.[42] Balaam's donkey who in the heart of the Bible uttered eternal words, spoke law and right, au-thority and property. What else did these gentlemen of the Enlightenment talk about before the fires of Saint-Domingue? And what passionate conversation was the "soul of the world" on horseback having with himself after Saint-Domingue had been put anew into chains? A conversation about right, the law, authority, and property.

But with the sovereign grandeur of the Enlightenment and what hovers at the peak of its reason, all this is no longer ex-pressed, as it was by Saint Augustine and his followers, in terms of eternal salvation, and in the interim, in terms of the simple management of everyday life, while "passing through" it. It is expressed from the perspective of a perfect immanence whose appropriate term is the death of everyone, the permanence of the law in whatever way it is presented, and of the sovereign who makes it at his convenience, but with his eyes riveted on the uncreated model of created nature. After which, each person is summoned to venerate the perfect layout of nature and the perfect good nature of the model that, its work done, withdraws into its corner, and catches himself hoping that his work does not drift in some unknown direction, into the hands of who knows which miscreants.

For the texts, conspiracies, and imprecations do contain a denunciation of heresy. It would seem that purely rational reasoning would demand that these criteria of belief and false belief be discarded. But what does one see instead? Not people rushing to the foot of altars to expiate the sins of others even as they chalk up rewards for themselves, but people fustigating, fulminating, welcoming, or banishing—and Rousseau knows a thing or two about that—depending on how the verticality of the relationship of all things to right, of right to the laws, of the laws to nature and to its maker, is exalted. In the background of all the good that is said about observation and practice in the most basic sense of those terms lies the constant need to be deferential toward this *dator munerum,* this "benefactor" whose truth has not been proclaimed or dictated but constructed and inscribed in nature. Science, a constant reference, is not the first but the second reference on a ladder whose topmost rung is occupied by a naturalness of truth. Whether progress is achieved through lengthy theories of observation or equally lengthy theories of syllogism, it always all ends up with this sacralization of truth, knighted by the transparency with which nature adorns itself in order to charm the person who looks at it in its splendid nakedness.

There are perhaps several ways of venturing this contemplation, this "theory." The Enlightenment authoritatively decided that the theory had never before been seen, and that it would shed light on its shape for the first and final time. Could that be the Enlightenment's own way of proclaiming in a single sentence the beginning—at last!—of history?

No matter what has been written about historicism accompanying this fantastic movement of thought, or the fun made of the German response, which seeks to anchor in the soil and subsoil a truth that is all too quick to make itself ethereal; no matter the force with which the case is made by people like Cassirer for an acknowledgement of the central role of historical thought in the Enlightenment itself, it will always be easy to object that historicism is a thing of the past and to point out that while it will reemerge in the future, the sacralization of the naturalness of truth, or of the realization of truth in nature, is in the meantime described here in the language, words, and images of Parousia, and not in the kind of tentative, provisional language that would be appropriate for the trial and error nature of experimentation, the fervor of research, and the bitterness of failure.

Voltaire is not alone in peppering the efforts of others with sarcasm when such efforts seem to him unworthy of the naturalness of truth. His jibes are remembered because they are right on target in all instances; his compliments are not. But it is easy to draw up a glossary of apothegms that people use to tear up one another. It will provide conclusive evidence to all of a canonical, priestly tenseness in all the great worshippers of nature.

Will it be held against me for thinking anew in this regard of Saint Augustine's techniques? The inventor of the philosophy of history makes way, in the heart of the societies that he describes so uniquely, for the path of those who "are passing through." He warns that "those who are passing through" could not care less about the institutional layout of the landscape that they traverse between birth and the afterlife. And each person owes it to himself to salute the openness of this great mind who declares himself open to all, curious about everything, and ready to listen to every little child who might have something new to tell him. But let others from the sect next door claim to be "passing through" between birth and the afterlife, following their path and not the one laid down by Saint Augustine, and you will see the Bishop of Hippo become suddenly impervious to any form of reasoning other than his own, retreat into a wall of rejection, and summon the police.

The quarrels and insults within and around the *Encyclopedie* were virulent and effective. So were the decrees (informal, of course) ostracizing people and expelling them from salons, and the measures depriving them of state income. Insults were not traded over the inadmissibility of the "protocol" of an experiment. They were, rather, all things carefully considered, over the lack of eagerness or punctuality in embracing what the thinking on the naturalness of truth and its political, aesthetic, and ethical drift could only "postulate."

Now at this "degree zero" of propositions and arguments, on what else if not on faith can the authority of the lampoonist be based? Posterity is a thousand times right to keep in mind the deep unity of this multifaceted thinking, and not to worry about the disruptions of the moment. Posterity is not wrong to detect in these upheavals that agitate daily life the old reflex actions of schools and movements, defending through contempt, rejection, expulsions what their arguments assume without proving, impose without first demonstrating. In the face of such defense mechanisms, faith and heresy literally make no sense, except, perhaps, when it all leads to Voltaire's exquisite tirades against the Capuchin friars.

So, once all this has been said, and one has hopefully mentioned what seems like perfectly standard murderous quarrels, one is obliged to return to one's own position, however weakly or firmly grounded in reason it may be, just like the neighbor's: namely, that of the comparison of these trivialities to the serious reality of slavery. What is the interest, the significance, and (on the planisphere of the naturalness of truth) the color of the continent of slaves and the sugarcane archipelago? The question is not incongruous. If it is, it is the only one to be so. And if such is the case, this uniqueness works in its favor. Congruous or incongruous, the answer to this question determines the meaning that will have been given to the interpretation of right, authority, and property—corollaries that derive from the truth inscribed in nature. On this major point, it is not forbidden to link together the French, German, and English elements of the same "illustration."

The blunt response, which overcame the enduring reticence of some, is of shocking frankness. Are you talking about Negro slaves? You can count yourself lucky if you are not referred to the theory of climates dear to Montesquieu. If you are spared that, you are invited to revisit your "anthropology," where you are treated to a catalog of muscles and mucous membranes that are classified according to their more or less remarkable porosity or dense viscosity. That too is science. Nevertheless, history will one day learn to consign this science's corollaries to post-Enlightenment prejudice, because as far as pre-Enlightenment prejudice is concerned, it had been inadmissible for ages, whatever the science that was invoked in its regard.

Let the *philosophes* stay in the salon, and that is perfect. The common people, whom Diderot needs and invokes, go to the antechamber, all ready to listen and understand. To the hospice goes the slave, and here and there, to the science laboratories as a subject of experimentation. Such then, when all is said and done, when all the beautiful speeches and various moratoriums are considered, is what, in the face of the ordeal of slavery, the egalitarianism of these gentlemen of the Enlightenment and the final word of their "sociology" boils down to.

But it would appear that not the slightest importance should be given to this "experimental" hierarchical system, which was fine for the Enlightenment and whose cruel consequences are borne by the slaves. One needs only read this laboratory hierarchical arrangement in light of the science of the period and its brazenness for everything to fall into place. For the slave, the expression "to fall into place" means, in this "scientific" context, to be nowhere and in the final analysis not to exist. Not to exist yet, or not to exist at all? We have had some idea about how this issue was settled. Fortunately, after the night of prejudice, came the dawn. But the sun does not rise for everyone. And dawn sometimes cruelly makes people wait, and not just in the winter in Lapland.

Perfectibility and Degeneracy

Dawn. Exactly. It came for Africa after having shown its face in the Caribbean. After coming to the rescue of some crowned heads and republics elsewhere, the French Romantic Republic—the second, that of 1848—transformed the slaves in our country into human beings, to use Condorcet's words. In the wake of these events, Europe, and France with it, also decided to recognize the humanity of the blacks in their lands. France expanded into sub-Saharan Africa, unfurling the flapping banner of the Enlightenment. Let's move forward in time. Goodbye Strasbourg, here comes Brazzaville. Gone is the introductory course on Gorée Island to the delights of the Antilles. The humanization of blacks is now done on the spot. And, of course, if in the era of transatlantic crossings people entertained themselves with the story of good old King Louis XIII, satisfied that the sweet epilogue to the abductions, barter, and the middle passage was baptism in the home of the good master and paradise as a bonus, in the era of high-speed subjugation, people were moved by the story of the humanizing delights of our civilization, touched by the grace of the Enlightenment—a lovely little story peddled by the din of cannons and the sweet sounds of mission bells. What delightful synthesis, intoxicating happiness for the black man: you work at home in an area exactly vertical to the paradise to which you will go as soon as your body is ready to provide manure to the soil. A little late, perhaps, but in vain, people will talk again about you, poor Negro, in a language bits and pieces of which your ancestors perhaps trapped to be sold off, had already heard in the death houses of Saint-Domingue or Louisiana.

Around 1930, Louis Bouiller defended a dissertation titled "*L'obligation au travail pour les indigènes des colonies d'exploitation spécialement dans les territoires français de l'Afrique centrale*" (The Obligation to Work by the Natives of Colonies of Exploitation especially in the French Territories of Central Africa). Its title leaves little doubt about its contents. Let's take a look at his concluding words: "It emerges from the above discussion that the native is in general totally perfectible, that he acquires relatively quickly the taste not for work, directly, but for the pleasures that work gives. Now, is this not the stage at which the vast majority of European workers are?" I can hear Sarraut exclaiming in Brussels in 1923: "French colonization is essentially a creation of humanity, a universal enrichment. This enrichment must be done and pursued in association and collaboration with the races that the colonizer governs and whose human value he must increase."

Increase human value. Create humanity. The perfect perfectibility of the native. I will not display the poor taste of digging into the filth of that section of French literature that celebrates colonialism by turning the savages into beasts, just as I have made a point, in the interests of mental sanity, not to examine what inveterate slavers in the eighteenth and nineteenth centuries thought of Franco-Antillean slavery. This "generally perfectly perfectible native," this "creation of humanity," this "increase in human value," are expressions—I have discovered—that were used, mouthed, glossed absolutely everywhere by the best, while African cavalcades were raising mountains of dust in the continent and—except for the punishment by cannons and kicks—a long time after imperial power had created innumerable Alsaces out there. These key words were everywhere, in the mouths of those who insist in the most humanitarian way possible on this indispensable "collaboration of the races."

Everywhere, those who talked this way took the Enlightenment for reference and absolutely swore by it. At the same time, they relied, and this is both sad and funny, on the know-how of missionaries, these retarded purveyors of prejudice, to teach the ABC of perfectibility to the perfectibles: patience, resignation, and obedience. And they all naturally found the magic word, the unavoidable, thaumaturgic word where it thrived: perfectibility, yes indeed. They used it endlessly, adapted it to all purposes with no hesitation, to the point where the expression "perfect perfectibility" became ludicrous, comical. To highlight this notion, which in itself alone was a whole project, they surrounded it with all types of observations on the state of degeneracy from which the natives should be rescued, with appalled descriptions of the degeneracy that awaited them should the colonizer delay in implementing the program of "perfectibilization." This was the level they had reached.

For anyone who is more or less familiar with contemporary thought, this is sheer sadness. Anyone, with a distinguished university education or no education at all, can tell you that this notion of "perfectibility" used so often by the Enlightenment, which created it, has nothing to do with the use to which the missionaries and the braggarts of the radiant epoch of the Native Code were to put it.[43] Let's be serious. With our eighteenth-century authors, perfectibility was nothing more than what it meant: namely, that man in society, whatever his behavior, is capable of doing better and is aware of this capacity, which justifies the existence and the action of all the other faculties that grace his nature. The corollary to this certainty, less forcefully expressed, can be formulated as follows: in society (outside of which no true humanity exists) man is capable of progress in the knowledge and development of his ethical and political abilities. Anthropologically accomplished, he has before him a whole world of qualities to know and to acquire—or to acknowledge and use—and this world is within reach of his reason and will. This capacity for continual progress in ethical and political conduct derives from his capacity for constant emulation in the area of virtue, no more, no less. Any interpretation of perfectibility that, in one way or the other, would seem to lead to some anthropology-like progression, according to which one group would place higher than the other on an ideal ladder—whose lowest rung is occupied by the Hottentot, the Eskimo, the Carib, and the highest by the European white of Biblical tradition—would be incorrect, out of place, and insulting to the theoretical legacy of the Enlightenment. So they said anyway.

Literary "Jules Ferryism" is woefully mistaken then in claiming to read in the Enlightenment a use of the notion of perfectibility that is conquering, anthropologically racist, and legally codifiable, and one on which France and her sister nations of Christian Blanco-land would have had every reason to base the philosophical and moral legitimacy of their gunboat African policy.

"Jules Ferryism" is not mistaken. If French thinking at the time picked up the notion—and its twin partner degeneracy, and their use—from the prevailing conceptual marshland, it invented neither the idea nor its manner of use. It simply took the dreadful initiative of reformulating in terms of a "sacred mission" and pedagogy what the Enlightenment enunciated with the serenity of an observation. But no special determinism is needed for a proof to be accepted. In history as well as in ideology, it happens that historians and ideologues stamp their words and ideas with the seal of evidence, even as they claim that the obviousness of the facts, innocent by definition, imposed themselves on them.

Let us be spared henceforth all talk of the innocence of perfectibility as the Enlightenment uses it. One has to be deaf not to hear, blind not to see the long acts of unreason that perfectibility accompanied, authorized, and imposed from the moment those less favored by nature or climate, geographical latitude or custom, appeared in the discussions of these gentlemen. On this subject, like in each of the important subjects discussed at the beginning of this study, the cantilena of perfectibility becomes annoying cacophony as soon as the less privileged—among whom is, if not the only one, the black man—appears right in the middle of the concert.

Let us proceed haphazardly. It is impossible to do otherwise, for the disorder is so great the moment one forgets, from conviction, method, or interest—certainly not from negligence—the irreducible oneness of the species, indeed the moment one only tries to describe the map of its various regions. Let's begin with Voltaire. He is a polygenist: for him, we are much too different from one another in this huge world for us to be all satisfied with the explanation of one Adam and Eve in the Garden of Eden. We are all probably first cousins but certainly not brothers. His conviction, against the current of prevailing thinking, must be solidly substantiated not to appear ridiculous. It is. The argument needs to dig deep into the most distant past of each man's ancestors. And it does. We learn that coming from diverse stocks, we were nonetheless—and each one of our groups in its time and place—all savages, all cannibals. That is the least of things. Nonetheless, human nature is one, and it distinguishes itself, wherever it shows up, by a principle of identity and differentiation. From the first, all races receive the priceless share of a beneficent instinct. Remarkable nature makes use of the second by endowing nations with "different degrees of genius" and with these specific traits of nations "that are observed as changing so little." In short, we are benevolent; only the faculty of understanding becomes refined in a nature that is always and perfectly the same. Conclusion? Depending on one's taste, nature is either perfectly logical or perfectly illogical, "which is why Negroes are the slaves of other men." And that is quite natural, one is tempted to add.

Buffon does not condemn slavery: he feels sorry for the misery of slaves, victims of the neglect by their masters of this humane duty of all civilized men to behave in a civilized manner. As is the case with Montesquieu, the principal scourge of slavery is that it endangers the virtue of those who administer it with excessive brutality. By neglecting this duty, by treating "Negroes like animals," the civilized man yields to violence and erects in and around himself—in the progress of the species toward its own perfection—the obstacle that is his own return to a state of barbarism. But is this "perfection" only ethical? Far from it. Let the matter be judged from the experiment imagined by Buffon to "rewhiten" blacks. A group of blacks is transported to Denmark. They are settled there. Care is taken that no interbreeding whatever takes place between their race and any other. They will multiply and become white! The only unknown in this obvious process is the duration of the experiment: "the amount of time it will take [the blacks in Denmark] to reenter human nature, and in the same vein, the amount of time needed to revert from white to black." It is clear here that man is white by nature and that he becomes black by accident (and we will see that with this accident, degeneracy occurs) and can only reintegrate nature by becoming white again. Consequently, should the process of whitening be confused with that of perfectibility, or does it develop according to its own rules? And while we are discussing that, what is the difference between this "gift of soul,"[44] referred to by Condorcet, and this "reintegration" that moved Buffon so much?

Does Raynal not speak, following Buffon, of the "degeneracy" of the inhabitants of America? Does he not take, both from Buffon and De Pauw, the idea of a "radical defect," of an "altered constitution"? It will take a lot of goodwill and bias, or a high dose of reckless irresponsibility, to place this "reintegration of nature," this "degeneracy," and this "alteration of the constitution" on the side of ethics, outside all anthropology—in the most abjectly racist sense of the word anthropology.

Let's bet once again on the innocence of these "proofs." It is easy to do so: all one needs to do is to forget the slave trade for a minute, the Black Code, and sugar. Let's bet. But preferably so that we can decide this time—after consulting Michele Duchet's opinion, the most informed on the question[45]—on the innocence or otherwise of the neglect. She demonstrates that for the Enlightenment, the white and civilized man is the best and perfect man, and she continues: "The idea of degeneracy of certain varieties of human beings within the human species hides a latent racism that later looks scientific and that finds a semblance of justification in the differences, then at their maximum, separating the savage world from the civilized world."

Let's remember the concern with scientificity in this matter, a concern that takes us back to De Pauw and more concretely to Buffon. Whatever the difficulty that he admits encountering in grasping the difference between a monkey and a Negro, the latter poses no less, and in total clarity, a separation between animal and man. Here, there is no involution possible by means of regressing over the threshold, whose layout is so difficult to make out. But working from this lucky find, Buffon establishes a hierarchy of men according to their "perfections" or "types of degeneracy." Thus the Native American is at lowest rung of the ladder. He exercises no sovereignty and has not subdued animals. Himself an animal of the first rank, he was to an extent where he was only by chance; he set foot on the earth but left no trace because he was incapable of transforming it or making it produce anything whatsoever. In contrast to the European, who invariably puts himself on the top of the ladder of perfections, the Amerindian is stupid, and his mind "lacks vitality and life." The Amerindians "lack passion for their females and as a result love for their kind."

Nevertheless one moves from the animality of the Amerindian to the perfection of the European. Not in one single movement, not in a rectilinear way: perfectibility will go through pauses, stagnations, setbacks; it will experience "moments of degeneration."

And how about the blacks? For a change they will not come last? But Buffon changes his mind. Within the human species, the two varieties whose features are the most removed from the model described for the whites of temperate climates are the blacks and the Laplanders. Is Buffon only thinking of shape and skin color? So it seems. He adds, however, that morphologically and chromatically, far, very far from the perfection of the standard, these "two extremes are equally removed from the truth and the good." Am I therefore justified in concluding from this that anthropology, physiology, and morphology were all contaminated by the notions of perfectibility and degeneracy that, I have been assured for centuries, only concerned the ethical and political activity of each person? But then it is pointless to spend an eternity on this: Buffon's authority was uncontested among these gentlemen of the Enlightenment. The quarrel (and which one by the way) over the notion of perfectibility has meaning only if it is peremptorily proved that this capacity is specific only to man, however rudimentary his reasoning or palpable his stupidity. In that case, why not welcome at a zero level of reason—the apogee of stupidity—the orangutans?

Because the blacks who associate with them (in quite a suspicious way, according to some—Bodin, for example) have, with full knowledge of the facts, settled the question. "The blacks, almost as savage and ugly as these monkeys, and who do not realize that to be more or less civilized, one must be more or less human, gave them a proper name, Pongo, an animal and not a human name." Irrefutable.

Let's exclude the orangutans, then, since the blacks exclude them. Let's mix Amerindians and blacks. Buffon concedes the faculty of thought to both groups. He knows they are both endowed with the power of speech: he detects in both "the germ of perfectibility." De Pauw does as much. Both combine this germ and its development with the unfortunate accident of "degeneracy" when it comes to comparing the black, the Laplander, and the Amerindian to the white-civilized-European (Christian, in short) standard: custodian of the norm not only in matters of beauty and shape but also—we remember—in matters of goodness and truth, of virtue, in other words.

I search in vain but cannot find in any of these considerations the seriousness of the much vaunted concern of not letting morphology, accomplished once and for all, be contaminated, if I can put it that way, by the degeneracy of the mind. I find on the contrary that the imbrication of the two is constantly implied, when it is not tirelessly repeated. Perfectibility and degeneracy are in play at all levels and erupt in the style not of individuals—as was anticipated in the enthusiasm of the commentators and the candor of philosophers theorizing their "varieties," whatever their claims to the contrary—but of groups, nations, and societies. The thinking on this issue and the terms of this thinking appear in the literature that is of interest to us only when conduct is compared to conduct, sociability to sociability, and production to production. But let the matter concern Rousseau and Diderot, let it occupy Voltaire, Helvétius, or Buffon, and you will see a diversity of descriptions of this perfectibility and degeneracy. One such *philosophe* will bless the creator for delivering nature to one man, accomplished by the very fact of being, whose aim is to approach indefinitely, with no misstep if possible, the marvel of the white man, to whose beauty "all the other nuances of color and beauty should be related." What if that man is already white? Then the matter is simpler: perfectibility becomes a matter of protection of and progress in the virtue acquired (a progress compromised in the white man who brutalizes his slaves beyond what virtue can tolerate). Another one will express his sorrow for man created naked and inventing language and reason but suffering under cruel determinisms that block his perfectibility at every turn and because of all sorts of unforeseen problems. Another one still, like Rousseau, seeing in perfectibility this faculty that "will develop all the others" depending on the circumstances, will also talk about the "decrepitude of the species" in connection with Amerindians. But let the black man appear, and invariably, with no notable exception, this pharmacology of the mind will describe him at the end of its analysis as it claims to have found him: rationally a custodian of the germ of perfectibility in auspicious days but still degenerate from a domestic, political and individual point of view.

In terms of Jules Ferry's doctrine, let's acknowledge how well these men could read. But on this basic theorization, who am I, Negro slave? In spite of my stupidity and simian ugliness, I am naturally perfectible. I perfectly am. By dint of my virtue alone (I like redundancies) I will go from undeniable stupidity to the most sophisticated mischievousness. Lazy, I will work. I will go from irascible and impetuous to meek and obedient. A thief, a liar, a dodger, honesty will henceforth be my norm. Wasteful, I will discover the virtue of savings. Insolent, I will learn respect. Vulgar, I will become subtle, even refined. Stammering, babbling, I will become a poet. A skirt chaser, I will become faithful. A poisoner, I will become an apothecary. A sorcerer, I will become an altar boy or a canon. In short, the germ of "perfectibility" will produce in me all the fruits that have for so long adorned the perfectible soul that has always inhabited the body of my lords and masters.

Raynal and Diderot believe in my perfectibility. They set it in motion. They want me to perfect my way of digging and planting. I will sow and shovel to the strains of melodious and delightful tunes or of some reed pipe, at worst. No drums above all, no drums. They want to introduce me to trade. I will be gently taught, with no hurry, to feel in my evolving soul and in my body, which, strangely, is becoming refined and hybrid, a passionate need to possess what the whites possess in abundance. I will continue to slave away but joyfully. A joy that will tarnish (but not extinguish, it is a question of dosage) the anguish of still missing what I long for so much and do not have as yet. I will continue to shovel away, blessing the generosity of my erstwhile masters, now my bosses, to the rhythm of my shovel strokes and my songs, punctuated by the music of my reed pipe. But I, formerly a piece of property in the Negro fair, will go to the market of knickknacks and twaddle. The gunsmith and the cutler will still be forbidden to me while my skin tone lightens up, my lips become less full, my woolen hair straightens out, and the deep valley in my deformed spine fills out. It would be a great pity if the mental, aesthetic, and morphological progress in my perfectibility were suddenly to bump against the degeneration of vice and tip into the ugliness of resentment and vengeance![46]

Perfectible, I am in the depths of my individual degeneracy and, if I could use a family expression, on condition that I am not mistaken on the model of perfection. All that is said about me in offices, salons, and boudoirs where my fate is of concern aims, I seem to understand, at getting me out of my simple function as a tool, an object, a piece of furniture, and at giving to this soul that has been awarded me, I remember, the finery with which the souls of whites improved themselves with no noticeable degeneration in a recent past, a soul that whites have from the moment of their birth: something with which to subject instinct to reason, to transform passions into virtue. The threshold reached by "whitItude," enables whites to develop perfectibility beyond this ethical, cultural, and "civilizational" achievement. As for me, I will still be at the stage of managing my instincts. And since, as I was saying, by progressing along this path, my path, my functions will become refined, my skin tone lighter, it will be child's play, with time, to make the distinction at one glance between the monkey and my companion, the monkey and me. But in the meantime, what is needed is patience.

Was this experiment of my rewhitening in Denmark, of my recovery up there of lost nature, this absurdity due both to Montesquieu and Buffon, imagined by someone at the height of the Enlightenment in political terms and not as an entertaining game of chromatics? Who else, apart from Condorcet—but we know with what reservations and cruel restrictions—thought of the experiment of recovery of my political dignity, which I must have once had, if the game of perfectibility-degeneracy is appropriate to me as to others? We are numerous in the Caribbean. We are even the vast majority there. The least that can be said is that we form a "variety" of humanity (in their language) that cannot be confused with others. We come from a common stock, and where we come from, we were a people (and that, Condorcet also readily concedes).[47]

Let them leave us alone to get on with our lives. A people we were before our dehumanization; a people we shall become. Unavoidably. The only unknown is: how long will it take us for our perfectibility—retracing in the right direction the reverse path taken by our degeneracy—to recover our capacity to exercise political sovereignty?

No, nobody wants this experiment: no more the Abbé Grégoire on one end of the spectrum than Montesquieu on the other; no more these two than the authors of the *Code noir* or the king who signed it. This experiment, which I have tried so many times and which so many times has led me to the pitchfork, the gallows, the fire, I will only finally pull off with Toussaint Louverture and Dessalines. But how strange: whether it fails or succeeds, the experiment will invariably be read as a sign of my irreversible bestiality, or my reversion to the state of bestiality. Whether they are moaning or not, the men of perfectibility rob me, out of considerations of justice, of the soul that they gave me out of mercy and pity.

Do I hear you say I am cheating? No problem, think that way. I stick to the texts with the scruples of a Benedictine monk deciphering parchments. Perfectibility leads each person in society to develop all his other abilities. Its decline leads to degeneracy everywhere, to the "decrepitude of the species" seen in Rousseau's Amerindians. I, the object, the piece of furniture, the pickaxe, I can hope for nothing other than the personal and domestic management of my instincts. I have lost sovereignty forever. I choose to conclude from this that I have never had it, according to this group of Jesuits who with elegance, generosity, and without the slightest scientific and conceptual risk give me the gift of whiteness that has been disfigured by the intensity of the sun but do not have the courage to envisage that political mastery can sprout, take root, and flourish in my "variety" of humanity.

Because this shift from one to the other and to yet a third of these three levels—the monastic, the domestic, and the political—is seen by the Enlightenment everywhere else in terms of perfectibility, with unfortunate obstacles. The articulation of perfectibility to virtue is again its work. For as far as I, a Negro thrown up in the Antilles, am concerned, all these philosophers are directly responsible through the errors of their rhetoric and the grandiose paralogisms of their picturesque babble for the blockage of this march toward goodness and truth, to talk like Buffon.

Article 1: "All men are born . . ." etc. Saint-Domingue perfected the expression. Constrained and forced, the France of the Enlightenment, the Revolution, and the Convention was to appropriate this expression after a few fires, and with the sword of Haiti in the aorta of its trade. In one single moment, I transcended the limits imposed on my perfectibility. In that same moment, I plunged to the depths of the abyss of my degeneracy to become a wild beast, according to them, although from my perspective, it was to invent my sovereignty with a bang.

A few more years and I will become food for dogs. Bull fighting has always entertained Spain, this mad country that offers the blood of bulls on a sand altar built to the ancestors. At the dawn of the nineteenth century, France invented "Negromachy" and offered itself in her country, the Antilles, the fashionable spectacle of my agony in the jaws of dogs.

Yes, food for dogs, in my country, in Haiti. And yet "perfectly perfectible," like my brother in the era of the Native Code, but a perfect degenerate, a Negro slave, an emancipated slave, a rebellious slave, a Negro in short. How moving this Enlightenment.

CHAPTER 3

Of Men and
(Under)Dogs

The Dogs of the Colonies

The problem then was settled neither by the music of reed pipes nor of flutes on the banks of the Niger. There was voodoo to start with and then drums and then things became more serious. Guns and iron spoke.

The blacks, who had risen up so many times, fought with such determination and fury that it could be said that in spite of the continuous massacres they suffered,[1] they had remained defiant and steadfast from the day following their arrival in Saint-Domingue and all over the Caribbean, until this night when Bouckman summoned the brave to torch and destroy the power of the masters. Fire is an old tradition of combat. Many centuries ago, Samson daringly used firebranded fox cubs against the Philistines and destroyed the latter. And how many slaves were there? How often did they not revolt—from Miguel the Avenger and Guiomor the Priestess in Venezuela, to Bouckman in the Caribbean, not to mention the daily and "widespread" flight of countless runaway slaves! Other names come to mind: the Valley of Blacks in Mexico, Ganga-Zumba in Brazil, Old Cudjoe in Jamaica, Mackandal in Saint-Domingue, Zan-Zan, Boston, and Araby in Surinam. They waged wars that sometimes lasted forty years. And to think that these "stupid" people are capable of standing up to the belligerence of their white masters . . . Sorry I'm straying; I promised to stick to issues concerning France and her slaves.

For what I have to say, it matters little that Bouckman's strategy appears starkly linear or subtly complex, that Toussaint Louverture's and Dessalines's, from beginning to end, now used blacks, now mulattoes, or again blacks suddenly freed from the mass of slaves, or indeed kind or wicked whites. I, a Negro slave, will not feel embarrassed by all the attempts made to denigrate my people's enterprise, the constant references to the twists and turns in Louverture's decisions and his many tergiversations. Now doling out compliments and begging, now casting insults and threats, now still allied with the Spanish, now with the French. I have only one answer, enough to silence anyone who wants to deprive me of my freedom. Let him think but a second of how other liberators used history to free their people. And if you find one, a single one, from the mists of time up to 1791 who did not dither, then I will temper my enthusiasm for Toussaint Louverture with some palinode on his inability to give me liberty through the subtle charm of a magician's wand. Even if this story of Haiti's slave revolt and of Louverture's epic struggle is given only two lines on the rare occasions when it is mentioned in French school history textbooks (books that are systematically silent on the century and half during which the *Code noir* was in force), it has been sufficiently discussed for me to consider it known, and therefore not to have to spend much time on it.

My concern is not with the number of cannons or the clever advances and retreats in battle. It is with the failure of the cowardly equivocations and the flagrant dithering of a universalist ideology stuck in francocentrism, and of a noisy philanthropy that thinks it has examined the problem when it has dealt with the imperial interests of a metropole that has since become a republic. My concern is to explain that if I struck at the heart of the institutions of slavery, it was not in anger against the Enlightenment but against the hegemonic claims that it promoted, advocated, and justified. My concern is with the fact that the Republic did not grant me freedom, which should have been the natural progression of its luminous logic, but that I had to wrest by force of arms the decree by which it had to acknowledge that this herd of monkeys was also an army of humans. My concern was the violent rejection of the "mercy" and "pity" of moratoriums; my interest, the passionate, incandescent conquest of my destiny. Now or never.

Now or never. Let's remember Toussaint Louverture. Let's understand him: the stinging nature of this alternative is not the guiding thread but the transcendent moment of his entire struggle on his island and of the later struggle that would exhaust him to death from hunger and cold in the prison of Fort-de-Joux in the Jura.

From this transcendent moment, I note a few episodes. In 1790, Saint-Domingue was rumbling. The rumbling of August 1791 did not accompany a clap of helping hands, but a hurricane of revolt. Two years later, on August 29, 1793, Toussaint Louverture imposed on Sonthonax the abolition of slavery in Saint-Domingue. On February 4, 1794, in Paris, "the enslavement of blacks in all the colonies [was] abolished." On 30th Floréal of the Year X (1802), the February 4, 1794, decree, was repealed—a period of twelve years in all from Bouckman to Napoleon, or if you will, from Bois Caïman to Fort-de-Joux.

The blacks did not invest the forbidden grounds of sovereignty singing canticles and fraternizing with their executioners. Their leaders stayed the course of "now or never": no more procrastination, no more concessions beyond those imposed by this imperative. The rest was simple. France was logical with her emancipatory, universalist, and philanthropic discourse. Saint-Domingue belonged to her. Blacks would regain real freedom there as they became human. Having acknowledged their duties, they would accede to the realm of rights through pathways and entrances prepared for them by France. And in any event, the abolition of slavery, wrested by the slaves and initialed without enthusiasm by the great nation, is only meaningful when viewed against the sacred rights of whites to property and the urgency to erect against the English and Spanish invasions the ramparts of bodies of legions of "soldiers of the Republic" still sore and scarred from the whippings of the master.

From 1790 to 1802, with pauses and movement, I set up camp right in the middle of the terrain of the law. But my right was a felony. I broke the chains and declared my law, while island and metropolitan whites counted and recounted their losses. The French Civil Code, after the Declaration of the Rights of Man and the Citizen, would translate the discourse of the Enlightenment into legal language. For me, who dared tear myself away prematurely from slavery and decided in advance my destiny and the political fate of yesterday's executioners and today's "collaborators," Napoleon was determined, through his actions, to do something that no one but me, perhaps, a free black, formerly a Negro slave, dared imagine: the blocking of the movement of history and the return to the bestiality of the *Code noir*. France sent its warships. I was attacked, surrounded, and put back in chains. According to some among them, I had finally become a human being. I was stripped of my humanity, reduced to my level, and promised the only thing that was due me: "mercy and pity."

And you, ferocious African, who triumphed for a while on the tombs of your masters whom you cowardly slaughtered (. . .), return to the political nothingness to which nature condemns you. Your atrocious pride shows only too well that

> servitude is your lot. Return to your duties and count on the
> generosity of your masters. They are white and French.

It is with those words that from 1802 Deslozières greeted Napoleon's decisions.

Will I be forgiven for dwelling briefly on the implications
in Deslozières's speech of the injunction "to return"? I return
to political nothingness by returning to duty, and vice versa.
I will easily push my impertinence to the point of celebrating
the logic of this Negrophobe. Everyone will agree that duty
without rights perfectly describes my "political nothingness."
And it will be held against me by all, wrongly but never mind,
for jumping from the atrocious Deslozières to the poets of
the moratorium and for accusing them, whatever the moaning that accompanies their words, of keeping me in a state of
political nothingness for as long as it suited them, as long as
they did not grant me full rights, all my rights. As poets, they
would have rather I renounced all revolt: they would have
done the rest. But in fact I have been standing since Miguel
and Guiomar even though the whites hamstrung me and bled
me to submission whenever I attempted to stand up!

Now the cannons of Leclerc were thundering away in
the ports of the land that I had saved by liberating myself.
Leclerc's huge armada, which came here to put me back in
chains, would fail. The frontlines of armies crisscrossed on
my island. Leclerc continued to press Napoleon to send him
ever more reinforcements. And it was in the violent conflict of
my "now" and the passion of France's "never" that the French
nation—that cradle of virtue and greatness, as it called itself—
invented the most sophisticated form of entertainment that
the slave-trading tradition had ever dared invent.

Cuba grew sugarcane. It practiced a strange form of dog
training. The mischievous and cruel indolence of an unexceptional slavery was replaced there with the brutality of slavery in the French manner as soon as the Catalonians, the last

to arrive from Spain, decided to grow as much sugar in Cuba as was cultivated in the French section of Saint-Domingue. The Catalonian slavers had a sense of irony, indeed sarcasm, but also affection for their French colleagues next door. This is because they feared that the wind of liberty would also blow toward their coasts and that their slaves would destroy Cuba as they had done Haiti. So Cuba took up the dog training trade: excellent animals to track runaway slaves. Monsieur de Noailles is a very important gentleman. His name appears prominently in all the brief accounts of the achievements of the Revolution. Monsieur de Noailles is a man of the Enlightenment. Does his name mean anything to you? But, of course, it does: he was the leading advocate of the "abolition of all privileges"; he was the embodiment up to that point of the sense of equality and more.

He was also responsible for the trade in dogs between the Catalonians of Cuba and the French of Haiti. When Leclerc's expeditionary force floundered in sickness and delirium, with Leclerc dying and Pauline Bonaparte in the throes of home-sickness, Rochambeau, full of himself and running wild, was governor of Haiti. His cruelty was unprecedented:

> The daughters of slaves were raped while still infants. While they were on this path, further horrors became inevitable. On holidays, Rochambeau began to throw Negroes to his dogs, and when the beasts hesitated to sink their teeth into a human body before the brilliant array of finely clad spectators, the victim was grazed with a sword to make the tempting blood flow. On the assumption that this would keep the Negroes in their place, the governor had ordered hundreds of mastiffs from Cuba. "We'll have 'em eat some nigger meat."[2]

As a Negro slave, I wonder whether it is proper to dwell on this nightmare. Whatever the cost to me, I acknowledge that I do sometimes forget the rape of my brothers' infant children because I am used to it, because I know the calm perseverance with which our white masters forced themselves on our wives, daughters, and young girls throughout the period of enslavement of my people in the Caribbean. Was my peoples' very animal existence next to whites not aggression enough against the fragile virtue of the masters, as Montesquieu the Bordeaux patrician and slaver in his spare time quietly noted, and Condorcet, the marquis, complained? So many others, slanderers, who dared versify the criminal flaying in terms of homage, would shake up many people. I am resigned to forget the cruelty of this aggression because I know it was widely practiced. I will go all the way, though, and ask my people to forgive me. The rapist—the French social cream surrounding Leclerc, Pauline Bonaparte, and then Rochambeau, the very man who treated me as an animal—knew at the moment of orgasm, and from the groans and tears of the little girl, that he was not holding a she-monkey or an animal, or a woman, but a child.

History—and I would not want to forget that fact now or ever—has meted out to my people the most spectacularly degrading death that the contemporary era ever invented in its early stages. I was thrown to dogs whose instinct was aroused by bruising me with the tip of a sword, if necessary, to titillate their muzzle with my blood. I was thrown to dogs on holidays, in the middle of the day, in front of the nation's elegantly dressed ladies and gentlemen, a nation whose armies were crisscrossing Europe and beyond, bringing enlightenment to dispel obscurantism and prejudice definitively, to sow the seeds of the cult of reason. But I was not even entitled to a "standard" execution. I was not entitled to burning by molten lead. I was not worthy of the macabre liturgy of hanging. None of these wonders invented by man's sense of beauty was appropriate for me, the animal. A pile of waste, a piece of meat, a smelling carcass, I am thrown to the dogs, because it was me, because I dared commit the ultimate crime. I, who am "nothing politically," invented my liberty and therefore created myself. I was thrown to the dogs for daring to negate this nothingness. Is thinking possible after Saint-Domingue?

Can I seriously retrace my footsteps and, from the bullring of this inconceivable "Negromachy," climb not as far back as to the theoretical excesses of dyed-in-the-wool slavers, which seems self evident, but to the equivocations of the supporters of moratoriums? I can and yet cannot: as usual, and for each of these disasters, it is a question of colors.

White, and whatever the tone of political color on my whiteness, I can hide behind the comfort of a thousand considerations and as many denials, sustained by many powerful thoughts on the timeliness of things, or deploy many powerful arguments on what is possible and impossible, depending on the social, political, economic, and commercial reality of each period. It is a tune whose stanzas and ritornello variations the reader and I know well. White and French by preference, I proclaim with total sincerity the good faith of the best of my people, and my conviction about the absolute aberration of such monstrosity. And yet, I did say they were perfectible but degenerate. And I even added the word "alas!" I did say they would one day, thanks to us, regain the true sentiments of nature, whose norms I decreed. I was moved by their "obvious stupidity," whose cause I attributed rationally to the masters and not to nature, thus making it possible for me to boast, at the height of the Enlightenment, of having made a sensational discovery. And that is: "The race of slaves is indolent, rebellious, unmanageable, and unsuitable for lessons in virtue, not as a result of a natural defect, God forbid, but of their masters' neglect and behavior toward them." Diderot? Condorcet? Jean-Chrysostome! I thrive on the Enlightenment, but I also know my classical writers. I took pity on the slaves' ugliness, which frankly troubled me. I have blackened page upon page to prove that they have a soul or that they could be offered one, but that was not an easy task at all. I filled pages and pages making clever distinctions between the bestiality of the blacks of Africa and the Negroes of the Antilles. Is it the fault of one group or the other? When it came time for a general assessment, I could not settle the matter definitively because the arguments were so finely balanced. It seemed unjust for me to plead their right to my justice immediately if that was to lead to the disruption of the white property-owning order whose scandalous injustice I have nonetheless denounced. I proclaimed their right to revolt. I even summoned them with paternalism and grandiloquence to rise up. In the course of the same sentence or the same downward movement of my lace sleeves, I explained how right it was to make fortune out there at the expense of their blood[3]—necessarily.

I often received dividends from slavers. I promptly cashed them. Out of virtue I kept quiet about it and discreetly contributed a few pistoles to some hospital fund for humanitarian reasons. I was not understood. The usefulness of the compromises was not adequately appreciated. Was the good-natured tone of my message even conveyed to the slaves? Was it even translated in a babble that was accessible, if not to their suspect minds, at least to the ears of these dolts? Alas, no! Was it properly explained to them that if they accepted my timetable of events and wisely acknowledged the unavoidable realities of the market, they would one day even taste of the serenity of political existence? Was the meaning of all this clearly explained to them? I fear not. They revolted too prematurely, too violently, and in too great a number. This was unfortunate. We were unable to support their awakening, and as was foreseen, they sowed disorder, killed owners, laid property to waste, and violated the most sacred of rights. Alas, we had to go back to the beginning—the calamitous result of their degeneracy. We had to start all over again at the point indicated by this scoundrel of a Deslozières, with whom I have nothing in common, and by this aesthete of a De Noailles, whose fight for equality among us, whites, people of good company, I loved so much. We had to start anew: at the level of political nothingness, of pure duty with, as a bonus—a substitute for these ever-present "mercy and pity"—the "generosity of the masters."[4] But to go from there to the spectacle of slaves savaged by dogs is a huge abyss. Or do you mean a small step?

If I am a black man, I will dismiss this beautiful rhetoric in two words: "On the pretext that a Negro is not a human being, the French made a slave of him, but when he reacted like a hero, they saw him as a monster" (W. James).[5] And do not think this is mere imagery. Toussaint Louverture was dying in his dungeon at Fort-de-Joux: from despair, of hunger and cold. Should he have received medical attention? With orders from above, his warders wrote the following report: "Since the constitution of blacks is totally different from that of whites, I sent the doctor and surgeon back, as they were of no use to him."[6] Let's be logical. Toussaint did not die. He croaked. A white man is killed or dies. A black monster is either thrown to dogs or dies like an animal. And yet people continue to think after Saint-Domingue.

Whether it is a matter of color or a simple matter of logic, the tiresome question that continues to be raised once De Noailles's dogs have eaten their fill and Louverture is dead is: "Who was responsible for the uprising in Saint-Domingue: Bouckman, Louverture, and Dessalines, or the Enlightenment?" More precisely, did Haiti make her revolution or did the French Revolution spread to the colonies? Let's start with the generous hypothesis that this question is "scientifically" neutral. It would seem right to respond that Haiti knew what was happening in France, that the blacks were witnessing the efforts of the colonists to keep their power and those of the mixed race and free blacks to be heard. That said, you can complicate the situation as much as you want, you will still not fully appreciate the agitation, drama, lawlessness, and executions that were taking place out there. Then do your best to rehash the good old story of the young Toussaint, who, a little older, is cast as well educated or illiterate (depending on the historian's viewpoint), reading and rereading the Abbé Raynal, dreaming over those pages (and only them) where Raynal and Diderot depict a black hero breaking free from his chains, rousing his people from lethargy, leading them to revolt, and systematically skipping those pages where the two partners wax lyrical about the advantages of trade and the exquisite beauty of the slave rhythmically digging away and joyfully ensuring the master's fat profits.[7] Imagine further the young Toussaint still dreaming, seeing himself as a black Spartacus joining at full bridle the men that Bouckman had fired up. Dare to take this short cut, don't be afraid: you will be perfectly in tune with official or, if you wish, ordinary thinking, whose framework is as moving and as Francocentric as they come.

Blacks could not possibly know the meaning of liberty or individual rights, and still less of equality or independence. Concepts are not spontaneously generated. They need the necessary conditions. These did not exist in Haiti but only among the French bourgeois and the enlightened aristocracy of the great nation.

Thanks to the literature coming from France and to His Majesty's courageous servants, the blacks learned and appropriated, with the results that we all know, a language and a system of values that they did not produce and could not produce. This has all been condensed in a single expression: The Enlightenment made Toussaint Louverture. It is in the nature of the victor to use all possible means to dispossess the defeated of his history. To Toussaint Louverture reading Raynal, with his finger on the right page and none other, is conceded the uprising but not its inspiration. As for the failures, they are not denied him. This then in broad outline is the francocentric theorizing of the slave uprising. There was no Haitian Revolution: there was only a Saint-Domingue episode of the French Revolution. What a radiant summit of the unstoppable rise of the Negro! Shackled, ironbound, starved, amputated, tortured, a runaway countless numbers of times, he needed Raynal and Diderot to tell him in some big fat book to free himself before he could think of doing just that. Without them he would have understood nothing of the irritation of the colonists. The eternal runaway did not know what freedom was: his perfectibility had not sprouted to that degree. Capable of hearing, perhaps of understanding, he was certainly still incapable of thinking for himself.

But we know the Enlightenment's tired contortions in matters concerning the slave. If he is as stupid as is claimed and lamented, how then did he manage the subtle academic exercise of deducing from a discourse that sometimes concerned him what that discourse neither overtly states nor suggests, and what it calmly and very obviously eliminates? How did he manage to snatch from the Enlightenment what the Enlightenment never dreamt of? Look seriously for Bouckman and Louverture in the Enlightenment. Look for Dessalines, the man who snatched Haiti from France. The Negro, always a slave and yet still standing tall, did indeed invent his liberty.

Are Haiti's black liberators going to be made, in spite of all the in spite ofs, the disciples of the Enlightenment? Fine, but then logic requires that things be clarified: these liberators subverted the language of the Enlightenment and gave it a meaning it did not have. Search in the language of the Enlightenment for the Negro—free on his land and sovereign on his territory. Rummage around relentlessly, you never know. Read, interpret, and twist the texts if they resist: they may end up yielding their secrets. On this point, Napoleon's reaction was right: he maintained French hegemonic rule and colonialism just like the Convention did, and shelled Haitian liberty to death.

Fortunately, it would appear that the France of today, of the bicentennial of the French Revolution is having a change of mind, discovering modesty and putting things in perspective . . .

The Men of the Nation

Putting things in perspective is something "The Friends of the Blacks" knew how to do without waiting for the obituary delights of the rare school texts to recall their struggle. It has become customary today not to pay attention to the casuistry in which the "Friends" excelled, and equally rare to pay heed to what they never abandoned: their axiom "white, therefore free" was meant to enable every mulatto to gain full entry in the category of "subject" or "citizen," and so much the better for him. All they had to do was turn to the *Code noir,* to understand its spirit more deeply, slightly amend the articles regulating the status of the newly born (free or slaves) by extending to the children of a free black man, through a strictly racial criterion, the privilege of being born free in the same way that a child born to a free black woman was born free. Please reflect for a moment on the predictable size of the number of these black or mixed-race children born free. The "scientific" program in this case corrected the legal aberration that consisted in perverting in the *Code noir,* by using skin color, a principle invoked by Roman law on behalf of the child of dubious paternity.

What then did Roman law stipulate? That the "fruit follows the womb." From this the *Code noir* drew the following conclusion: to a free womb, a free child; to a slave womb, a slave child, whatever the status of the penis. Let's add in defense of Colbert and Louis XIV that they did not invent the perversion of the principle: they simply took it from the best authority possible: Saint Thomas Aquinas.[8] Will it be said from now on that the "fruit follows the penis"? Without taking into account the fact that the abolitionists would lose on the one hand what they gained on the other, such a proposal would not enjoy the support of the legal tradition invented to compensate, thanks to the obvious "sedentariness" of wombs, the wandering tendency of the penis. The "Friends" will put it better: the fruit follows whiteness. Could they say that? Yes, science came to the rescue of the law and, once again, of philosophy.

Science, we know, posited a perfect correlation between "whititude," perfection of the species, and freedom. It proclaimed, with an impressive battery of arguments, the superiority ("flagrant," or "all things considered," that was the unimportant "point") of white over black. It advanced an interminable and unbelievably dense explanation for the "biological" capacity of "whititude" to redeem and bring to perfection the blood, juices, and flesh with which it was mixed. The "Friends" liked this kind of science. It quite naturally led philosophy to the conclusion referred to earlier that the smallest drop of white blood that mixed with black blood, infused in this blackness—henceforth seen as purely accidental and skin deep and therefore frankly negligible—not the promise but the realization of white perfection and liberty. Science therefore corrected the law at the right moment, and the "Friends of Blacks" could, with this formidable ally, fight for the emancipation of all mulattoes whom they hoped (they wrote it hundreds of times) would control, once their interests merged with those of whites and of empire, the pure Negro slaves; control them with a firm and strong hand that would delight the pure whites when the scales would have finally fallen off the latter's eyes! The generally rich mulatto would become the ideal executive of the sugar industry, the dreamt-of policeman of white order. Such was the strategy of the "Friends" from beginning to end. Such, after the rhetoric and in the hour of truth, was their liberating and at the same time colonialist program, the one that the clumsy Bouckman and Louverture and others were later to ridicule. Such was their language. It is worth reading their writings. They are accessible to all.

Could the thinking of the "Friends" have been different from what they wrote or said? Nothing prevents me from believing it could, nor does anything force me to believe it could not. You say they thought differently. So be it. In that case they concealed their thinking very well because in their statements, numerous texts, and countless "addresses"[9] they explain and embrace without the slightest scruple or reticence this theory that we shall call scientific or racist, with or without quotes, or even racial, if one is sensitive to the beauty of compromise.

All this has been forgotten today. The "Friends of the Blacks" are the friends of all the blacks and are the nice guys of history. The others are the scoundrels. Matter settled.

That the others are villains is not in doubt. But the pure black slave may very well not be content with this rough and ready division and may still want to rummage not in the villainy of the scoundrels, which is patently clear, but in the kindness of the kind, whom he has the right to be suspicious about, if he chooses to.

Let's go back a bit. It was before De Noailles's dogs, before the farce of the abolition of Year II,[10] a little before the explosion of Saint-Domingue, which sent the "Friends" scurrying into hiding.

I have mentioned Condorcet a lot. It seems unavoidable to do so again. He was the best (haven't I said it enough?) and was ahead of Grégoire only by a short distance. We have read his *Réflexions* with as much impartiality as possible. They are often disconcerting. But that book predates the dawn of the Revolution. History often came undone in the mad rush that we all know about, and the Marquis had evolved. Not by himself alone. The antislavery debate imported to France from England was taking shape, so to speak, but there was nothing really grand about it. Speeches in favor of emancipation were becoming more urgent than before the eruption of Saint-Domingue. In the fiery heat of passions and the revolutionary virtue of the Convention, the "Friends," and Condorcet with them, were making the case over and over again. For general emancipation? No: for the simple and imperious need to end the slave trade, to emancipate the persons of mixed race, and "to control" the blacks. Until the day when Condorcet paused and clobbered the representatives of the free nation with the argument about the impossibility of combining two declarations of faith that are as mutually exclusive as water and fire.

The issue facing the representatives of the nation was whether the planters of Saint-Domingue should be accepted as deputies or not: as planter-deputies intent on representing their class, that of the mulattoes and the few free blacks, and becoming the legislating body out there for humans, "sub-humans," and "monkeys." That they would legislate in a manner commensurate with their appetites was self-evident. Condorcet ridiculed them, calling upon the Assembly to witness the radical contradiction between the two declarations of faith: that of "deputy of a free nation" and of "planter." This double profession of faith later enjoyed a brilliant career in the world of the first literary stirrings of some privileged French adolescents (the majority of the nation could not care less, even today, about the Republican destiny of the blacks of that time and are completely ignorant of the episode).

One reads them, becomes indignant, and blesses French genius. From their rhetorical punch, it can be deduced that the "deputy of the free nation" deserved to share with Montesquieu, without the shadow of a doubt or suspicion, the laurels of antiracist and antislavery sentiments.

Crown him then. But also give yourself the trouble of reading, in the flights of rhetoric that precede the double profession, what Condorcet also says to the deputies:

> "The Society of Friends of the Blacks" dares then hope that the nation will consider the slave trade and the enslavement of blacks as one of the evils whose destruction it must decide on and prepare, and it thinks it can confidently address the assembled citizens to choose their representatives and denounce to them the crimes of violence authorized

by the laws and protected by prejudice. We know that
there are injustices that cannot be repaired in a day and
that, tied to political interests or seemingly so, can only be
destroyed with the care necessary to ensure the good without having to pay too high a price for that good. *We are
therefore not asking you now to vote for the actual destruction of this evil.*[11]

What precedes and what follows is grandiose. But is it really
the reader's fault if he detects an elegant distinction between
the urgency to "destroy slavery" and the time to "prepare the
destruction of slavery"?

Try doing a simple reading of the two professions of faith
after that, and try telling the slave, the one with pure black
skin, with no European blood in him or in the DNA of his
soul, that nothing the history of the "Friends of Blacks" taught
him gives him the right or obliges him to add to the other two
declarations of faith a third, which pettily calculates the limits and the significance of so much mercy, so much pity and
parsimony for justice.

The planter's declaration, very truthful, remains that of the
perfect slaver. That of the deputy of the free nation displays
the brilliance of the Enlightenment in white major. The third
presents the rainbow-like charm of compromise between the
radical nature of the principles and the cowardly strategy of
colonialism and moratoriums. The third, of course, I have
made up entirely. But I am not drawing its parts from my
imagination. They fit into each other in my mind now that I
have read and calmly digested the passionate literature of the
"Friends" and Condorcet. The requirements of reason can be
read in the first declaration, the petulance of sarcasm in the
second,[12] and in the third, reason will be seen disguising itself in deceit and rubbing on itself the oils of the "perfectibil-
ist" compromise, whose sweet scent will still embalm slavery
throughout the time period required.[13]

Profession of faith of the deputy of a free nation	Profession of faith of a planter	Profession of faith of the "Friends of Blacks"
I. Liberty is a right derived by every man from nature and cannot be legitimately taken away for all time from anyone, if he has not been convicted of a crime for which this punishment has been applied.	I. Liberty is not a right that men derive from nature, and society can legitimately reduce men to slavery, provided some of its members benefit from it.	I. Liberty is a right that every man derives from nature and of which society can legitimately deprive a mass that is subjected to slavery for a long time, on condition the nation decreed that the peace of a few must take precedence over the exercise of this right.
II. Any infringement of one of man's natural rights is a crime that cannot be excused by the financial interest of those who committed it.	II. If the financial interest is fairly substantial, it can justify any infringement of human rights, any barbaric treatment, even murder.	II. Any infringement of one man's natural rights is a crime justifiable by the political interest of a nation on condition such a justification is made while "moaning."
III. Property must be sacred, and society has no right to seize arbitrarily any individual's.	III. Society has the right to force a class of men to work for the profit of an other class.	III. Property must be sacred, and society has a duty to protect the property created by slaves for as long as is necessary in spite of the fact that they were arbitrarily seized by their masters.
IV. A man cannot be another man's property, and consequently, Asian despotism is contrary to reason and justice.	IV. A man can be another man's property, and consequently, Asian despotism is neither contrary to reason nor to justice.	IV. An inferior being can be his superior's property as long as the inferior has not risen to the latter's level. Consequently, justice and reason can find accommodation with Asian despotism.

V. All citizens must be subject to the laws and enjoy protection from them.	V. The law can tolerate in one class of citizens the violence and crimes that it severely punishes in another.	V. As long as public order requires it, the law can tolerate against slaves the violence that it punishes against free men.
VI. Every man's conduct must comply with justice, even if it is against his interest, and it is despicable to sell another man's liberty for money.	VI. Justice is only required to the extent that it is consistent with one's interest, and it is quite permissible to sacrifice the liberty of others for one's fortune.	VI. In a free nation, the interest of the slave is to conform his conduct to the justice of the white man, and it would be impolitic not to compensate the masters adequately for the loss of their slaves.

Am I right—as a Negro slave awaiting the redemption of the people of mixed race and happily looking out for the day when the white man and the mulatto will tell me in unison: "Your turn, now"—to see and expose in this third profession of faith the letter of the charitable hope of the "Friends"? This right, history has given it to me, and I will take it.

At Twilight: The Enlightenment by Day . . .

During the day, the Enlightenment is invoked. One keeps warm by the glow of its lights and prepares food with its heat. So much the better if one is the right color. So much the better if one has one's napkin ring on the right table given that the story of the Canaanite woman happened only once.[14] One needs daylight to see hues and colors clearly, daylight and background lighting to discover under the beautiful uprightness of truth the reptilian obliqueness of lies. Night is another matter.

At the height of the Enlightenment, of the *Aufklärung,* Herder, the German philosopher, advanced a vision of a philosophy of history whose very Augustinian theatrical conception delighted Hegel, who plundered it copiously without the slightest acknowledgment. Goethe's teacher, Herder was recognized, beloved, and protected when necessary by his student; a frightened witness to the dangerous drift that German culture was taking and to the growing dominance of French thought, taste, and aesthetics, he could only interpret Enlightenment universalism in terms of an invasion, and philanthropy in terms of the enslavement and subjugation of everybody to one person. He read things this way because he believed in the irreducible reality of the existence of peoples in their plurality, and he could not but shudder to see the growth, at the doors of a fragmented Germanness that was inefficient in its quarrels and stuck in its archaic enterprises, an organized, coherent, structured, and single Frenchness. He was neither, as is sometimes written, and as one might want to read him in this regard (when he is read) the eulogist of the savagery of nature the better to pose as the denigrator of cultures, nor the brute of the *Sturm und Drang* and nationalism, nor the rhapsodist of the fevered passions of a romanticism spewing out its venomous anger far from the salons where the servants of reason were speechifying. He is nothing of all that. He quite simply and rigorously reflected on the anchoring, necessarily geographic, of all forms of cultural specificity. He described cultural spaces and the stages of the history of thought in terms of an arborescent development (whose most fascinating illustration he claims to find, like Goethe, in Spinoza), as the deployment of a system with a thousand entrances that preserves its mystery everywhere and that tightly regulates history according to the rhythm of the lives of men who both rule it and are ruled by it: childhood and adolescence, maturity and old age, death and rebirth. In his eyes, the French thought of his age did not represent the childhood of something new but the aging of an idea that was drawing to its end and whose collapse into death would give rise to something that no one could predict, an idea whose decay, he feared, would feed the rhizome of an empire that would mean the death of peoples. Herder who, in philosophy, refused to play Sybil found himself playing Cassandra, and he was frightened. A visionary, Herder viewed with trepidation the very thing that filled Hegel with enthusiasm: reason on horseback dressed as a braggart, the spirit of the world galloping over all the roads of Europe. Satisfied and fascinated, Hegel prostrated himself in spirit before the emperor who killed Louverture, exacerbated slavery in Haiti, and threw human beings to dogs.

But before all that happened, Herder watched colonial France act and speak. He could not have been more correct when he noted the tragic contradiction involved in singing the praises of equality and philanthropy, in ridiculing serfdom in Europe where the industrial machine had seriously started to replace human hands while at the same time maintaining slavery in the colonies, where the slave was supposed to be cheaper than the machine. Herder took note, highlighted the fact, and moved on. Along the way, he unleashed a fitting compliment—"Flatterers of this century"[15]—to the thinkers of a modernity that is so expert at maudlin philanthropy or physiocracy and at singing praises to excessive wealth accumulation by machines here and by slaves there.

Herder did not care to make distinctions: the flatterers are the men of the Enlightenment on this side of the Rhine, and the men of the *Aufklärung* on the other side of the same river.

Two hundred years later, contemporary French political thought seems to deserve the same compliment. And to justify its use, one does not even need to spend time evoking the contemporary administration of a moratorium (the last?) in Kanak country, whose conditions cannot be compared without impertinence to those elaborated in the past for other lands but which must be mentioned if only out of decency.

Watch how contemporary thought deals with the great questions of the day. It does this by first softening their rigor through the systematic application, as poultice, of that thick paste of grandiloquence and mercantilism, which transformed into lumps the transparently beautiful language of the Enlightenment each time it had to speak of the liberty, dignity, and humanity of others. Our progressiveness finds the means to talk about our "others" only if those means coincide with a "consensus-on-essential-things" attitude among the general public, which itself is nothing but a sign of our essential lack of a fighting spirit. We remember everything about the Enlightenment: its magnanimity to bend its century to its will; its small-minded pusillanimity not to endanger the smallest portion of its economic gains whatever the arbitrariness involved in achieving this, or the wars waged in the lands of others; its clever mix of solemnity in the proclamation of the rights of our country and of sonorous moans when it comes to comparing its dignity to that of other peoples, its rights to those of others, the imponderable value of its life to the value of the life of others.

As good disciples of the great school, inexhaustible on the rational need and historical urgency for the advent of a world without injustice, of unquestionable equality of rights and obligations, we invoke time constraints with papal seriousness; we invoke the unavoidable and unforeseeable iron laws of politics, the harsh laws of the market. Exactly like them. And we concede to the staunch sharks of economic liberalism the only thing that they ask us to concede: that the time for debates is over and that the time for every man for himself has arrived.

Here we innovate. Do we for sure? Every man for himself? The expression can be interpreted in the selfish and narrow-minded sense in which managers of wine bars of ideas use it. But we refuse to do that. We leave that kind of selfishness to them, and they know it. But it can also be understood in the sense of the nationalist egoism of the managers of "eternal values" and of braggarts. And there, whether we are dragging our feet or rushing off, we have no problem meeting our charming enemies exactly where they expect us. They exclude, we exclude.

Do they count immigrants? We do so with them. Do they shut down their borders? We padlock ours. Do they practice a policy of promotion or subjugation of such and such a region in the Third World? We honor that policy when it is our turn to rule. Do they provide guns and gunpowder according to the law of supply and demand, as if they were displaying our melons in foreign markets? We do exactly like them, when those who claim progressive credentials operate cash registers and order books.

But where we are unbeatable, where we have learned from the Enlightenment not to confuse the beauty of grand principles and the parsimonious charm of their implementation is when we debate endlessly—whether on the invitation of the sharks or the progressives—on how the "foreigner" accedes to Frenchness. On our official forms, we simply call that obtaining "the honor of being French." We talk endlessly about the rejection experienced by applicants in other countries. We despise, if need be with panache, the methods put in place by other nations for the same process and the ideas they use to justify those methods. And we insist on the colossal, historical fiction that in our country the right to citizenship through choice takes precedence over the value of citizenship through bloodlines or birth. We insist on the truth of this fiction about "free choice" and expect each candidate applying for the honor of French citizenship to reflect on this honor and to be especially careful not to reveal that what matters to him are his interests and not honor, about which he could not care less. Let him dare reveal his true intentions, and we can assure him of the nation's anger. Convinced by the Enlightenment that virtue is integral to Frenchness and that one cannot opt for one without the other, we want his decision to be driven by virtue and not mere interest, which smacks too much of bread and butter considerations.

Each person, on the Right and on the Left, defines virtue in his own way, and thank goodness for that. But each wants it present in their camp. We hardly use contemporary ideological explanations, if at all, to define it, press it into service, or embellish it. But we rediscover the consensuality of the Enlightenment and its techniques of exclusion and procrastination when it is time to congratulate those who overcome the obstacles, to encourage those whom we condemn to continued waiting, and to console those whom we reject forever.

All differences considered, if we wanted to adapt the mystique of the two declarations of faith about blacks and slavery discussed earlier to the problematic of immigration and naturalization (let's forget "integration")—the last avatars of the debate or absence of debate during the Revolution on the humanity or nonhumanity of blacks—we would certainly be successful. Here, too, we would easily set out the perfect declaration of "a deputy of a free nation," whose rigor would delight us. We would also do a pastiche of the declaration of the "planter" that is the diametrical opposite of the previous one and whose vulgar brutality would disgust us. But here again, "the deputy of the free nation" would whisper at the right moment, which is to say now—and to the authorities concerned, to the government of the great nation—the compromise of a hybrid and, consequently, admirably consensual declaration.

Two hundred years after the storming of the Bastille, the leap backwards that is so fashionable today in our country—from our repudiated theoretical positions to those that we currently hold—does not have the innocence of a summer evening's whim. We flatter our century as these gentlemen flattered theirs, with the difference that they made their century, whereas we endure ours. But to give ourselves the illusion of making our century all the while practicing the holy virtue of consensus (this kind of thing that could be described as the secularization of a "holy communion"), we retain, in our references to the Enlightenment, the Revolution, and their aftermath, the words and actions that made for good relationships even if that meant disaster, and we cover up the icons of those people whose uncompromising standards led to conflicts. We have quite simply erased revolution from the Revolution: let us embrace, mad city, the great upheaval that was but a night of love.

Do I really need to give details? I am not thinking of the Vendée but of the crucial test of the "flatterers of this century": the chains broken here but kept in place there, the industries created here, and the slavery maintained there. We call this calibration of chains and the niggardliness in breaking them, our sense of moderation, concern with efficiency, and calm attachment to the achievement of the possible. Moderation, efficiency, and the possible were all combined one day by history, that prostitute, with "Negromachy." This feast was not foreseen, but it occurred all the same. Not only after the Enlightenment, but also because of the criminal delays—because they were so consensual—of the servants of a language that was universalist and egalitarian in its ideas but regionalized and hierarchical right from its earliest formulation: too bad for those from elsewhere and those at the bottom.

If this meaningless word "postmodernity" is to mean anything at all, it would probably mean, when applied to thought as well as to architecture, that when there is nothing new left to say or build, or nothing left to say and build in a new way, one builds and talks only through a montage of citations. "Postmodern," the flatterers of this century quote from the Enlightenment. They quote it well, I must admit. They are puffed up with its spirit, they get bogged down in the logic of its rejections, and they drown in the tragedy of its indecisiveness.

All the same we are not yet at the stage of the dogs of De Noailles, but we are already at that of the barking of Le Pen and his hounds. And these are all the more resonant as our sense of proportion, of efficiency, and of the possible in the administration of justice and injustice for those who did not choose to be born on the right side of the tracks, to quote the song, explain our daily limping and open the door to the possible advent of fearfully effective excesses.

"But these are Negroes. They should wait; their day will come," said the Enlightenment.

"But these are immigrants. They need to wait; their day will come," we say between two references to "human rights."

Wait for what: the dogs, the wolves? During the day we invoke the Enlightenment, we bask in its brilliance. But what if one is black? For blacks, the night is more suitable. They meld with it perfectly. And the brilliance of the Enlightenment quite naturally becomes lunar pallor on their skin. It is the time for incantations, charms, and cold wind. It is also the time for certain popular and festive activities, of the most beautiful parades, and the most fashionable social events.

. . . And at Night

Three nights in 1989: in June, July, and December. The first was the night of the "pals," the second, the night of the masses, and the third, that of the leaders. It happened in Vincennes, at the Champs-Elysées, and in the Panthéon, in other words outside the walls, in the city center, and in the holy of holies, respectively.

Toussaint Louverture's name helped organize the first night. The pals fixed their rendezvous. They met, rejoiced, got dazed and drunk on rhythms and sounds. They danced away their joy to be together. They expressed with mouth and body their hatred of hatred, their rejection of exclusion, and their contempt for contempt—all under projectors, in front of giant screens, and in the right environment. Those who inundated this night of June in the year of the bicentennial with their music, cries, and passions are those from below. The pals did not beat about the bush when the moment came to set the tone at night. They signed up for the night, not out of "instinct" but after careful thought, and stuck on their posters next to the little hand the picture of Toussaint Louverture or his simple profile. Whose head is that? The message was not clear enough. The poster contained two lines of explanation. Legible? Let's say they were. Was it then possible to know how the poor man's adventure had ended? Oh no! It was possible to know that he had *served the French Revolution and the spirit of the Enlightenment.* It is as simple as that, and no one is going to make a fuss about it. The two lines explain Toussaint's dark skin and his allegiance to the Republic, which alone transformed the Negro slaves into human beings, and that's it. A strange shortcut that, in the universally consensual beatitude of this bicentennial and its spin-offs, foregrounded Toussaint's submission to the Republican state, relegated to the background his strategy of emancipation, and extinguished under the cold ashes of neglect the embers of the memory of his revolt.

Could one do any better in a single night, for this night? It is difficult to say, judging from what could have been gleaned about that night from the displays of the previous days. Let's not talk about the symposia or the scandalously little time spent discussing slavery and its abolition in the many roundtables, meetings, chitchats, and scholarly proceedings that were devoted to each and every aspect of the periods before, during, and after the Enlightenment and the Revolution. Let's say nothing about the place devoted in this endless fiesta of conferences to a reading of the Haitian events that is sympathetic to the thesis of black historical initiative and French resignation. Let's forget, out of decency, that no national radio station or television channel found it appropriate in this bicentennial year to remind its listeners through a word or an image—not even between the weather forecast and the sports page—of the anniversary date of the uprising of Saint-Domingue, of the vote of the Convention abolishing slavery. That is understandable. The glorious and the remarkable had to be sorted out from the ephemeral and brought out of the silence befitting the insignificant and the unremarkable. In the middle then of this universal silence,[16] to talk like the Enlightenment, could the pals do any better that night than what they did in a single night?

The answer is clearly no. How else could the pals have known these things other than through "erudition," this old marvel that disappeared with prejudice? They were told that Toussaint Louverture was black, part African, part Caribbean. It could not have come at a better time. He was a bit of the ancestor of all the pals, an ancestor whose crime was to have had the wrong face and be unlucky. He was black and nice, black and brave, brave and republican; he was for consensus and was not vicious. And the pals danced outside the walls not knowing what their leaders knew, and about which they gave a simplistic summary on their posters. They danced that night in weak homage to the weakest episode of one of the greatest revolts of our history and theirs too: that of its defense.

In the ministerial antechambers, it was now possible to point to the brilliance of that night in response to all those grousers who dared suggest that the Republic had not deigned to commemorate the memory of the man who snatched the decree that propelled the Enlightenment well beyond itself, by finally putting the Republic, in spite of itself, in harmony with the law . . . for a time.

Did the Republic cheat this time? It never cheats on serious issues. It is happy to let those who do not have a clear understanding of matters of rights and citizenship to get excited outside the walls. It is generous. But because it is above all just, it summons the people to the heart of the capital to celebrate wildly as they are wont to do, with arms dangling and as onlookers, the superb procession of its glory in the middle of another night, in the middle of the night of nights.

July 14, 1989. The Champs-Elysées became the glittering scene of a classic slapstick comedy. The Enlightenment, and the image of its successive bursts of brilliance in the four corners of France and the world, was hoisted on rolling floats and paraded. The people were asked or forced to read through their misty eyes the grandiose that lay beneath the burlesque, the magnanimous beneath the sarcastic.

The night suits blacks well. On condition they wear makeup that renders them visible in some way. The France of the bicentennial had the supreme audacity to train and parade two mounted spectacles of blacks in makeup and to order a crowd of more of them in military procession.

Two mounted spectacles. One featured a black character attired in tuxedo, gesticulating at a chorus whose sounds were barely audible. Below the character in tuxedo was a stage decorated in red and flooded with light. There, a group of black female dancers crowned with wreaths of almond-tree flowers and adorned in immaculate white colors that fit their complexion as feathers to a swan sketched out rather unsteadily some dance steps, tried some entrechats, and laughed at the buntings on their float. The float, with clear geometrical structures, well-rounded curves, meticulous ridges, staged the artistic and social whitening of blackness, the example of a perfectly successful training. Everything—from the fake sumptuousness of the décor, the reddish brightness of the silks, the dazzling whiteness of the dresses and crowns, to the abject stupidity of the imposed roles—insulted the dignity of blacks touched by the grace of the Enlightenment, in Diderot's or Jules Ferry's version of it. By the Enlightenment and the cannons. But how accurate! Perfectibility and commerce, whose wonders these philosophers and physiocrats had prophesied, indeed culminated in the solemnity of this umpteenth insult to blacks, in makeup in the middle of this night of nights.

How can the journey traveled, from the first barter of "ebony wood" to the last African cavalcades of the nineteenth century, be measured for the ordinary mass of onlookers if only its final destination is celebrated? Republican France owed it to itself to show the people that road's layout. It did.

And the onlookers, seeing the soldiers of the southern continent proudly parade in their red uniforms and in headgears that were part miter part kepi, were able to relive the emotions of their school memories or pappy's stories. These soldiers were the way, soldiers whose wounds—and the good pleasure of whose white bosses—they had used four days earlier as safe passage to escape from the status of outlaw of the "Native Code" and enter into that of citizenship. No, the bicentenary processions did not commemorate the disasters of an endless colonization. No, it made no reference to Galliéni's wretched actions in Madagascar, for example, or to the absolute humiliation caused by the "Native Code" first in Algeria and then in sub-Saharan Africa. To impress the ordinary onlooker, after the doggies and the dinner jackets, in this journey backward through time, came the soldiers—many and sumptuous and by rank. The Republic lends beauty to what it touches, dresses up those who serve it. The message is clear.

This path of servitude had had a beginning. The people have the right to grow ecstatic in the contemplation of their icon. And they were given it in the commotion of the second "Negro float," the float of Negroes before the kiss of the colonist and the tight embrace of the Republic. In a pile of muscles, in a mad arborescence of arms and legs diving into the night from all sides, were the blacks. Gone, here, are the finely measured ridges, the geometrical order, and drastically reduced curves. Was it an organized arrangement, a pile, or group of people? It was a pile, a jumble of members, of muscles, of bodies that culminated in the figure of a corpulent giant pounding away at an immense drum with his fists. The pile yelled, gesticulated, in a wild mix of animal skins, fabric of some sort, and the uncontrolled display of arms and legs. Darkness in the night: the savage in his excesses and intemperateness, in the vanity of his being, in the delirium of his flesh and the emptiness of his mind.

The onlookers liked it. The newspapers the following day

all spoke of the crowd's enthusiasm during that night of celebration of the Enlightenment. *Libération* asked for a repeat
performance. A repeat of this celebration where France, not
satisfied with the pleasure of flirting in the African scenes of
its passacaglia, with the old tradition of a kinship between the
black man and the monkey, by clearly bestializing the pre-
colonial period (represented by the pile of humans), pushed
its arrogance to the other extreme, an extreme that, if perhaps
fascinating, is undoubtedly racist, one in which France reduced to insignificant dwarfs, with arms, breasts, and lips of
stunning beauty—it recognized herself in each—the various
peoples of the world that were touched by the Enlightenment
and its guns. Like the Iberian people, reduced to a baby torero
caressed on the cheek by France—an act by which the French
think themselves absolved forever of the carnage wrought by
the Napoleonic wars and the War of Spanish Independence.
But we were speaking of blacks, in the darkness of the night.
How about Toussaint Louverture? Haiti? They were good
for the pals, outside the walls. In the heart of its capital, the
Republic displayed its arrogance, magnified its greatness.
In the same breath, it transformed its crimes into a blaze of
glory, forgetting those who propelled it well beyond itself. It
adorned those that it reduced to vassalage with the most beautiful colors. It forgot itself, made them up, and failed to realize
that by proceeding this way, it had grandly crossed, as might
be expected, and with what success, the threshold of what is
bearable in the contemptuous. It no longer realized—what an
imbecile—that it was casting insults deep into the hearts and
souls of those very people whose destiny it thought it was celebrating with this nocturnal procession.

The success of the Enlightenment simplistically conveyed
to the ordinary people from float to float is clear: the blacks
were nothing; France made them into human beings. From
the bare-chested giant sporting pendants on his ears, brace-
lets everywhere, and towering over a mass of people, to the

gentleman in dinner jacket surrounded on the stage by female dancers, lies the path of perfectibility that leads you,
savage—through submission and obedience in your army
uniform—from your rowdy nothingness to the most precise
design of the most perfect of our outfits: the standard of humanity. Contemporary readers of the Enlightenment know
how to interpret in their own way the ancient story of the old
man who must die in order to give birth to the new man. It
is a touching exegesis, a refined synthesis of the prejudice of
the previous day and of today's dogma. Could today's taste be
better flattered?

Yes, I know. A black woman all draped in the colors of the
French flag sang, belted out, the "Marseillaise." Ask those of
her complexion whether this lady, draped in her sacred majesty, this lucky aesthetic find was singing of consensus, allegiance, or revolt. The night of nights was, for blacks, the clear-
est illustration of the vulgarity of Hugo's statement: "Ham is
a monster. Ham is nobody. The southern continent is empty.
God has given it to you, white people: Take it."[17] The lights
were turned off, the streets were swept, and night was chased
away by dawn.

Leaders and their retinue are not in the habit of carousing
with pals or mixing with ordinary people, whom they summon to act as sycophants along prestigious avenues where
generals and entertainers unfailingly march. Leaders need
platforms or balconies and an entirely different, affected cere-
mony. They need style and class and, if possible, concepts.
Leaders adore concepts. They use them. So the high and
mighty of the Republic, both of letters and the arts, of industry, ethics, and socialism conspired, and all found themselves
occupying the best spots, the best seats in front of the temple
of virtue: the Panthéon. The bicentennial year was going to
die off quietly. It had to be brought to an end with some serious business, definitely funereal in character, but majestic and
virtuous, before Christmas when the little Jesus returns—as

he has now done every year for the past many centuries—to occupy the stage with the ox and the donkey from the middle of December to New Year's Eve. So a little ahead of the solstice then, the year's events were concluded, events celebrated in an atmosphere of consensus and with the slogan "we're all good, we're all nice." The leaders went up to the holy of holies and "pantheonized" Monge, Condorcet, Grégoire.

"Black from head to toe," Monge's canonization leaves me indifferent. Whites will one day explain his merits to me if they so wish. I will listen as usual, try to understand, and certainly be satisfied that such a great man merited the ultimate recognition of his own people after waiting for almost two centuries.

What can I possibly have against the "pantheonization" of Condorcet and Grégoire, and on the basis of what right? In their day, these men fought "the good fight." Grégoire, Condorcet, Monge: these are, Mr. President, the three men you have chosen. "Posterity honors the dead who speak to their hearts and minds," the minister in charge of the bicentennial said to the president. The minister went on to catalog the merit of all three, the rigor and integrity of their struggles. One would need a good dose of bad faith to point to the absence in the official speech of any reference to Grégoire's and Condorcet's compromises with the inhumanity of slavery, even if such compromises were temporary and designed to save the white order and the empire. One would also need a good dose of pettiness to deplore the absence of any reference to the distinctions insistently made by these two men between absolute and relative blackness, between abolition now, later, or never.[18] I plead guilty to this bad faith and pettiness. In the homily that night, a lot was said about women, Jews, and the equality of rights and education for all. But just like during the night of the people—when Negricide took the form of a grotesque parade, and Napoleon's destruction of the Iberian peninsular begun, ended, and lasted just long enough for an affectionate cuddle between the torero dwarf and Merrie France—so the night of the leaders took up the issue of the abolition of slavery in a single phrase for the sole merit of the Republic, and in it, for Condorcet and Grégoire. A single sentence was sufficient. One needs to reread the minister's speech to see its many inaccuracies: it states that slavery was abolished "fifty years later" (sixty would have been closer to the mark); it situates, for the attention of the leaders, the foundations of Condorcet's and Grégoire's struggles exclusively in French thought—the sempiternal Enlightenment—and associates Haiti with the history of abolition only as a reminder of the grief that struck the island on the abbot's death. No amount of interpretation or reinterpretation of the speech will reveal anything different in it: the slaves count for nothing in this narrative; they ask for nothing; Toussaint Louverture does not exist; his name is not welcome in those places where courage and virtue are celebrated.

I have the right to conclude from this that between leaders, every effort is made to stick to the white premises of white logic, if one is to avoid blundering into God knows which conclusions. No, I have no right to involve either the Negro or the person of mixed blood in the story of the abolition of slavery, the privilege of whose narrative the Republic intends to keep to itself, either to distort it or tailor it to its needs, regardless of history.

The minister then referred to the sad end of Condorcet ("for Condorcet . . . the mass grave") and the Abbé Grégoire ("forbidden to anyone to administer the last rites to the old man guilty of acts of Revolution"): "Receiving you in the Panthéon is an act of reparation," he added.

To be systematically silent throughout this entire evening at the Panthéon, where every word is carefully weighed, nothing is left to chance, and where we are reminded that our Republic set itself the equality of rights and knowledge as its new frontier; to be silent—in this context of ultimate homage to Condorcet and Grégoire—on the Haitian revolt and Louverture's: is that the way to serve "the equality of rights and knowledge"? Do Antilleans and Africans not have a right to their memory? Is being silent on these names not the leaders' way of using a discourse that serves their objective: law and order in the streets, white law and order in history? One is entitled to cry as much as one likes about Condorcet's and Grégoire's sad end and to approve of this act of "reparation." But unless the leaders are guilty of crass ignorance, which is unlikely, aren't the rhetorical contortions that one needs to inflict on oneself not visible enough? Contortions needed—at the very moment when the unfurling of each sentence makes the banner of "the equality of rights and knowledge" flap under the Enlightenment—to better cover up the official silence on that other sad end, the one that in Fort-de-Joux swept away Toussaint Louverture into nothingness.

During this night in the Panthéon, the minister quoted a passage from a speech delivered five months earlier by the president in the Jeu de Paume. It is now my turn to draw on the president's words:

> We are gathered in this hall in the Jeu de Paume to reflect together, before the country, on what binds us to this past, and to better conceive our future task. A people without a memory is not a free people. Dictatorships start by erasing from history facts that they deem awkward in order to bar access to the past. And believing themselves masters of the future, they muzzle all rebellious thoughts and words.

Here no rebellious thought or words are muzzled. We are not in a dictatorship. Nevertheless our very Republican leaders gave proof "before the country," in the most dazzling of feasts, in the most prestigious of places—the Jeu de Paume and the Panthéon—that they can, in the most democratic way possible, hurt the liberty of a people and its basic right to know by manipulating memory and erasing "awkward facts from history." Like his minister in the Panthéon, the president succeeded in narrating, in the Jeu de Paume, the real end of slavery, well after the death of the Enlightenment, without once mentioning either the revolt in Saint-Domingue or Toussaint Louverture's name, but that of France alone!

Epilogue

In 2089, there will also be a night of the leaders. The man who forced the abolition of slavery on Enlightenment France, on revolutionary France and on white rights, and who paid for this with his life will enter the Panthéon. That night, there will be a leader who will be moved by the sad end of the giant. He will proclaim, I think I can hear him, "Toussaint Louverture, receiving you in the Panthéon is an act of reparation." This will happen just before Christmas, during the high point of the tricentennial anniversary.

The leader of that period will recall with superb lyricism the frontiers that the Republic set itself a century earlier: "the equality of rights and knowledge," the "eradication of racism in the hearts of men," the rejection of "all exclusion." He will reflect on this equality, abolition, and rejection. And then he will gesture grandly toward the catafalque: "Come in, Toussaint."

Three nights. From Vincennes to the Panthéon: a century? This is no longer than the moratorium imagined by Condorcet for the slave's emancipation. Meanwhile, what if our historians of the Enlightenment started by encumbering it with its poverty? But that presupposes that the France of leaders, of philosophers, and of historians will get rid of their chauvinism. Will a century be long enough for that?

Alas! I cannot reasonably envisage a shorter time period.

Notes

Preface

1. "Those concerned are black from head to toe and have such flat noses that it is impossible to feel sorry for them. Little minds exaggerate too much the injustice done to Africans. For if it was anything like what they claim, would it not have occurred to the princes of Europe, who sign so many useless agreements, to sign one in their interests out of mercy and pity?" Montesquieu, *The Spirit of Laws* (Book XV, Chapter 5), trans. and ed. by David Carrithers (Berkeley: University of California Press, 1977).

2. Hegel explains (in *Reason in History*) that Africa has no history and that it is in its nature not to have one. Victor Hugo, in a speech delivered on May 8, 1870, to celebrate the abolition of slavery wrote: "Africa, what a land! Asia has its history, America hers, even Australia has one that goes back to its beginnings in human memory: But Africa has no history." What is Africa to Hugo? "A mass of sand and ashes, an inert and passive pile, this monstrous Ham who by his size blocks Shem (. . .) a land of excessive heat and darkness" (extract from the same speech). I will return to this point at the appropriate time.

3. Reissued by Louis Sala-Molins as *Le Code Noir ou le calvaire de Canaan* (Paris: PUF, 1987).

4. Herder was a German philosopher and theologian and contemporary of Goethe. He will be discussed at length later (see chapter 3, the section "At Twilight").

1. Condorcet, "Lamenting"

1. Michèle Duchet, *Anthropologie et histoire au siècle des Lumières* (Paris: Maspero, 1971).

2. "Let us declare slaves movable assets" *Code noir,* art. 44; and see above, note 3.

3. Condorcet, J. A. N. de Caritat, marquis de: *Réflexions sur l'esclavage des Nègres.* Par M. Schwartz pasteur du Saint Evangile à Bienne, Membre de la Société économique de Bxxx, Neufchâtel et Paris, 1788.

4. Ibid.

5. As Christ said . . .

6. . . . and as Marx said.

7. All these choice measures, and those that will be quoted throughout this chapter, are by Condorcet (op. cit.), whose moratorium must presuppose in some sense the suspension of the *Code noir,* which could not have anticipated them.

8. ". . . by lamenting over this kind of forced consent that we have to give to injustice" (op. cit.). Besides the quotes, all references to style are taken from *Réflexions.*

9. In the *Code noir,* the king refers to the colonists as subjects, and to the slaves as chattel of the colonists. The slaves are not "subjects of his Majesty." Legally, their status is that of property, money, livestock.

10. See chapter 1 for a summary of Michèle Duchet's work.

11. Has Zeus not deprived me of half of my brain? We shall consider the advantages and disadvantages of this amputation as we proceed.

12. Condorcet belongs to that group of physiocrats whose abolitionism can logically be deduced from a calculation of the economic disadvantages of slave production. All the same, abolition

must be achieved in the long run, because as a good physiocrat, he believed in gradual change.

13. Bartolomé de Las Casas, monk, bishop and indefatigable and exemplary defender of the cause of Native Indians, conceded to each human being (we will examine the implications of this concession now and later) three types of sovereignty that he sees as constitutive of that person's humanity: monastic sovereignty (my right over myself), domestic sovereignty (my right in my family), and political sovereignty (my right in the body politic).

14. Condorcet, op. cit., and chapter 1, note 7.

15. The doublet in which, it will be remembered, Montesquieu's so-called antislavery position culminated (see preface, note 1).

16. We will examine later Diderot's and Raynal's suggestion (in *Histoire philosophique et politique du commerce et des établissements des Européens dans les deux Indes,* Paris 1772. Choice of texts by Yves Benot [Paris, Découverte, 1981]) that slaves be made to work in step as a way of fighting their melancholia and increasing their production.

17. In *L'An 2440* (Paris, 1770), Mercier prophesized a reign of freedom for blacks, and the political hegemony of slaves following their revolts and emancipation.

18. Spain imposed on its black slaves the scrupulous observance of a series of steps in the process of whitening and stipulated that if by the sixth generation the rise was achieved by the rules, "the mulatto would be considered white." The *Codigo negro carolina,* a Spanish avatar of the French *Code noir,* was written in Santo Domingo in 1784. The absurd regulations on whitening disappeared from the (Spanish) royal edict of 1789.

19. Hobbes's views on man's violence and brutality before the contract are as familiar to all, as are Rousseau's on man's goodness and gentleness before the contract.

20. Bartolomé de Las Casas, cf. chapter 1, note 13.

21. Spinoza distinguishes three kinds of knowledge, from the grossest to the subtlest. The subtlety of the subtlest is of such . . . subtle subtlety, that merely to describe it is to put it beyond the reach of all ordinary mortals but Spinoza and Christ.

22. There were fastidious and endless quarrels among theologians

and philosophers on the dividing line between blackness and bestiality, blackness and humanity. The fastidious corollary to this was that if the black man's humanity was problematic, to say the least, then the soil he inhabited could not have legal reality (law being a business of humans). What was clearly meant is this: Blacks may live in Africa, but Africa is not their "homeland," as they cannot constitute "peoples," and vice versa. A lovely point of view, backed, as we saw, by Hegel's genius and Hugo's kindheartedness.

23. Again Condorcet, op. cit., both here and in what follows.

24. Spain, with its centuries-old experience in the practice of slavery, had created the job of "general protector of the slaves," with one protector per district, province, or colony. The protector did very little. But he at least had the merit of being there.

25. "For a century, there has not been a single example of punishment inflicted on a colonist for the murder of his slave." Condorcet, ibid.

26. By comparison, the Spanish Black Code (which deals with slavery in the Spanish colonies as we noted earlier; see above, note 18) calculates that with three years of work, the slave would have been worth its sale price. So it is pure profit after three years. But why waste time on such details? Condorcet's thirty-six years show his pure generosity, his moving morality (the Spanish Black Code and the *Réflexions* belong to the same decade). The emancipatable black at thirty-five has been working and tasting of the whip since he was seven or eight. So, do the arithmetic yourself, and divide into three, it is not difficult. Compared to the Spanish Code, Condorcet, without moaning this time, allows the master a 900 percent profit! Quite a bundle.

27. Historians and lawyers have drawn a lot of attention these past few years to the exemplary nature of Condorcet's struggle for the normalization of the legal status of Jews and the recognition of the rights of women to full citizenship.

28. A long scholarly tradition, misguided and corrupt like so many others, sheds light on the curious consequences of the division of humanity and the planet made by Noah two days after the flood and on the eve his memorable booze up. To Japheth's descendants, he bequeathed the northern Mediterranean and the West

(clearly, the West which one day will be heir to the entire Revelation). The blanco-biblical people are the Japhetites. To the descendants of Shem, he gave the eastern and southern Mediterranean. Among the Semites are the Jews, through whom is transmitted the message of rejection of the New Testament. It is all touchingly simple. To the children of Ham and his son Canaan, he gave slavery and that nowhere of a place, Africa. Noah condemned the children of Ham to be the slaves of those of Shem and Japheth forever. When it comes to piling on Africa, the exemplary and inveterate anticlerical Victor Hugo readily pitches in with his thunderous references to this divide.

29. Servet was burned alive not by the roman Inquisition but by Calvin, the Inquisitor.

30. Exodus 21: 2 and 21: 26–7; *The Spirit of Laws,* Book XV.

31. *Le Code noir,* Article 13: "It is stipulated that if a slave husband marries a free woman, the children, male as well as female, take the condition of their mother and are free like her irrespective of the father's servitude; and that if the father is free and the mother a slave, the children are similarly slaves."

32. See preface, note 1. Contrary to received wisdom, Book XV of *The Spirit of Laws* does not provide a condemnation of slavery in general but only critiques the abuses of a practice that should be regulated but not eliminated. Significant in this regard are the titles of chapters 8, 12, 13, 17, respectively: "Inutility of Slavery *among Us*," "*Abuses* of Slavery," "Danger of the *Great Number* of Slaves," "Rules *to Be Made* between the Master and the Slave" (emphasis mine). On Montesquieu's position on this subject, see my edition of the *Code noir* (see preface, note 3). Other traces of Montesquieu's pro-slavery sympathies will be noted as we proceed.

33. He deserves this description. His financial links with a slave-trading company would suffice to justify it, even if we did not have this project of reform of the slavery of blacks that is Book XV.

34. *The Social Contract* (Book I, Chapter 4) condemns all the forms of slavery examined by Grotius and recalled by Rousseau. The " totally novel" case of the triangular trade and the Euro-African slave trade of his time (already omitted by Grotius) does not figure on the list. Not a word is said about Euro-Afro-Caribbean slavery

in the *Discourse on the Origin of Inequality.* Not a word anywhere else. It is really not enough, a point to which we will return to in the following chapters.

35. See, in connection with the attitude of these gentlemen, Michèle Duchet's classic work cited above.

36. The image is Mercier's *(L'An 2440).* See above, note 17. Diderot and Raynal use it in *L'Histoire philosophique et politique des deux Indes* (see above, note 16).

37. By a decree dated 1786, the king limited to fifty lashes what the slave could receive from the master at a time.

38. Available to French-language readers are two magnificent works by Bartolomé Las Casas: *Très brève Relation de la destruction des Indes,* and *Trente Propositions très juridiques* (Paris-La-Haye: Mouton, 1974).

39. Need I recall the fact that in 1793 the slaves of Saint-Domingue forced the abolition of slavery on France with arms? That the revolt had begun there two years earlier? That it was only in February 1794 that the Convention abolished slavery for reasons that remain very murky? But we will come back to these issues in chapter 3.

2. The Market of Equals

1. At a conference jointly convened by Germany and France, the European powers and the United States of America, without quarreling, gave themselves, in Berlin in 1885, the right to partition Africa, even as they condemned slavery.

2. By *The Native Code* is meant all the set of laws by which colonial France kept the "native" in its colonies at good legal distance from "the citizen." The elements of the Code form a harmonious whole (or, rather, different wholes, one for each colonized zone) from the middle of the nineteenth century to the end of World War II.

3. Two flights of lyricism among many others in the calm blue skies of French colonialism:

Jean Jaurès in 1881: "We can say to these people without misleading them that France is loved wherever it has established itself, that she is missed wherever it only passes through; that wherever her light shines, it is beneficent, and that where it does not shine, it leaves behind a long and soft twilight to which eyes and hearts remain attached."

Léon Blum, in 1925: "We accept the right even the duty of superior races to pull toward them those who have not attained the same degree of culture, and to ask them to join in the progress accomplished by science and industry."

Both citations are from *L'Etat du Tiers Monde* (Paris: Découverte, 1989). See the section "Perfectibility and Degeneracy" in this chapter.

4. Author's emphasis. (Translator's note: For an English translation of the Declaration, see Lynn Hunt, *The French Revolution and Human Rights: A Brief Documentary History* [New York: St. Martins Press, 1996], 77–79.)

5. We saw aspects of it earlier when we accompanied the Negro to court, where because of the *Code noir,* he found the door shut in his face, and we realized that Condorcet did not intend to open it for him. We are grateful to Jean-François Grossin for a reading of *Réflexions* (in his 1990 master's thesis in political philosophy, University of Paris I) that is as rigorous as it is stimulating—a thesis that we very much hope will be published.

6. Mirabeau is an abolitionist. The "Friends of the Blacks" are abolitionists. Reading their "memoirs" closely, one notices that the destiny of mulattoes concerns them much more than that of Negroes, and that the precise curved shape of field Negroes is of greater concern to them than the immediate emancipation of all slaves. We will return to the political significance of these racialist, if not racist nuances. Back to Mirabeau: scholars talk a lot about his abolitionist stance, and their point is taken. But it would be preferable to examine this abolitionism more closely to see if it went any further than the others'. What does he say? That France's political and commercial interests require the progressive and gradual emancipation of slaves and the immediate end to the trade; that the slaves, introduced progressively to receiving wages and to the prospects of freedom, would produce more and better. Unstoppable like Condorcet in ridiculing slavery, the great orator was never short of means when it came to imagining how to administer in slavery the endless end of slavery. I am grateful to Silvio Zavala for permission

to refer to his unpublished *Tres aceramientos de la Ilustracion francesa a nuestra historia* (Mexico, 1989).

7. Rousseau, in *The Social Contract,* Book 1, Chapter 4, demonstrates that since he is nothing, the slave cannot possess anything. With Rousseau, it is a question here of highlighting the absurdity of slavery. The *Code noir* rules out the granting of an allowance to the slave. The Spanish *Code noir* regulates the granting of an allowance, but through a legal trick of total perversity, it deprives the slave of all control over his money and transforms this bonus into an obstacle adjustable to the emancipation of the slave.

8. See the section in chapter 3, "The Dogs of the Colonies."

9. See above, chapter 1, note 34.

10. Schoelcher advocated (with passion) that after abolishing slavery, France should penetrate Africa and subjugate the Africans to its interests.

11. 1789: The Declaration of the Rights of Man and the Citizen. 1794: the abolition of slavery. 1802: the reestablishment of slavery. 1848: the final abolition of slavery and the technical implementation of the decree.

12. See chapter 1, note 32.

13. Valladolid. We have to put an end one day to the myth of the disappearance—with the emergence of feudality in Christendom, in white Christendom—of slavery and with it of serfdom. Slave trading routes remained all over Christian Europe. Little used after the beginning of the transatlantic slave trade, they only finally disappeared a long time, a very long time, after the discovery of the Americas. See, in this regard, the irreplaceable Ch. Verlinden's *L'esclavage dans l'Europe médiévale* (Bruges: 1955 and 1977), a book whose title does not do justice to the extensive range of its research.

14. We owe to Feuerbach the most luminous philosophy of man that Western reason has ever produced. His books, of which *L'essence du christianisme* (Paris: Maspero, 1968) is among the most read, is one of blinding passion controlled by dazzling genius. See chapter 3, the section "At Twilight."

15. Let us understand by that the ring of church language when the language mixes, law, ethics, economics, politics, and canon law.

16. The theme is everywhere in his work.

17. It is known that for Aristotle, natural slavery exists (*The Politics* I, 3–7, 1255b).

18. See the section in chapter 3, "At Twilight."

19. Clearly, from Montesquieu to Hegel.

20. The young Negro child as a "domestic animal" in the smart homes of those who flit about the Court is one of the least discussed consequences of this little discussed triangular trade. See, in this connection, C. Biondi, *Mon frère, tu es mon esclave* (Pise, 1973), and *Ces esclaves sont des hommes* (Pise, 1979).

21. Rousseau, *Discourse on the Origin of Inequality.*

22. J. Lafontant, *Montesquieu et le problème de l'esclavage dans L'Esprit des lois* (Sherbrooke, Quebec: Naaman, 1979); Gabelli and Morize, ed., *Correspondance de Montesquieu* (Paris, 1914). See, while it awaits well-deserved publication, Laurent Estève, "Montesquieu: Le livre XV à l'epreuve de l'esprit des lois" (master's thesis in political philosophy, University of Paris I, 1989).

23. Contemporary historical research notes the late appearance of the idea of the child as a subject worthy of specific interest in our civilization. The issue here is that of a specific conception of the child, of its conceptual autonomy, if I can put it that way. More clearly put: when does the child cease being "something other" than a miniature adult? The real interest of the approach is clear. But if the pedagogical, hygienic, and aesthetic identification of the child vis-à-vis the adult is late in coming, that surely does not justify an anthropological rejection of the young of the human species.

24. *The Spirit of Laws,* Book XV.

25. See in this regard the indispensable books by Carminella Biondi referred to previously.

26. See Michèle Duchet, op. cit.

27. None more than the Abbé Grégoire paid greater homage to Las Casas's relentless struggle for the recognition of the rights of Native Indians and his merciless critique of the murderous drift that the conquest of the Americas had taken.

28. Las Casas waged the battle on the theological, legal, and political fronts. Claver sacrificed his life caring for and healing the wounds of the slaves in their death houses.

29. See Las Casas, op. cit., and see chapter 1, note 13. Let's briefly

recall his positions. The Native Indians constitute peoples endowed with political sovereignty, which they exercised up to the arrival of the Spanish. They are men that fully enjoy domestic and monastic sovereignty; they are not slaves. Natural slavery does not exist, and Spain cannot advance any serious arguments to deprive them of their states and reduce them to slavery. On all these points, adds Las Casas, "the same holds true for Blacks as for Indians." Las Casas's argument is a direct reply to the Aristotelian theory of natural slavery, and a constant reminder of the unity of the human race as it is presented in the biblical story of the Creation. Not once does Las Casas accept, even in passing, the traditional explanation of a slavery deserved by blacks—seen as the descendants of Ham and Canaan—as punishment for the fault of their "common father."

30. See the section in this chapter "Perfectibility and Degeneracy."

31. In the language of the Enlightenment, the "science" of theologians constitutes prejudice par excellence.

32. *The City of God,* Book XVI, chapters 8–9.

33. Matthew, 15: 21–28. *The New American Bible.* Wichita, Kans.: Catholic Bible Publishers, 1993/1994.

34. Paul, *Epistle to the Romans.*

35. That authority goes from God to king "through the people" ("auctoritas a Deo per populum") was already a conviction shared by Thomas of Aquinas. Of course, the notion of "people" remained vague.

36. In this regard, Voltaire is unstoppable. So are the encyclopedists.

37. To read the philosophies of Descartes, Leibniz, and Spinoza without their theological underpinnings has been very fashionable for a long time. But in philosophy is fashion equivalent to "sufficient argument"?

38. The expression on Descartes is Pascal's.

39. Punished by his people for the crime of miscreance.

40. He left in order to escape from the censors and their censorship.

41. We owe to Spanish neo-Scholasticism a new way of formulating the law and the relationships between sovereignties. Vitoria Suarez and Molina (among others) are names that the ordinary

French reader very rarely encounters in his readings but that were central to European thought from the sixteenth to the seventeenth centuries.

42. Hegel saw Napoleon on horseback in Jena. He had a rush of emotions. He saw, he confided, "the soul of the world" on horseback. The "soul of the world," working through the inspiration of "the world spirit," had firmly reinstituted the slavery of yesteryear in the Antilles.

43. See note 2 in this chapter.

44. Ame. See chapter 1, the section "Animal, We Will Give You a Soul."

45. Op. cit.

46. Raynal and Diderot, *Histoire,* in Benot's choice of texts, quoted above in chapter 1, note 16.

47. On the other hand, the Spanish *Code noir* emphasized the point without proposing a model of slavery that was any less monstrous than that imposed and managed by France.

3. Of Men and (Under)Dogs

1. From 1528, Spain promulgated one decree after the other to put down the slave revolts.

2. Alejo Carpentier, *The Kingdom of This World* (London: Gallancz, 1967). Translation from the French excerpt is mine.

3. I am thinking of Diderot. I could just as well have been thinking of Raynal and would still be right.

4. I humbly ask to be forgiven by Montesquieu and Deslozières for lumping them together in a single sentence.

5. C. L. R. James, *The Black Jacobins: Toussaint L'Ouverture and the San Domingo Revolution* (London: Allison and Busby, [1938] 1984).

6. Ibid.

7. See chapter 2, the section "Perfectibility and Degeneracy."

8. In Thomas, the form determines and qualifies the existence of the composite "matter-form": the womb, whose "form" is to be a slave, cannot produce a child whose "form" would be liberty. It is as simple as that.

9. Unavoidable reading in this regard is the very beautiful collection of texts collected in *Révolution française et abolition de l'esclavage* (Paris, 1968), 12 vols., 99 titles in 4 series: Slave Trade and Slavery, The Society of the Friends of Blacks, Revolt of Blacks and Creoles, New Legislation.

10. The abolition of slavery took place in Year II (1794).

11. This "address" appears on p. 163 of the collection cited in note 9 of this chapter. Emphasis mine.

12. Both are by Condorcet (see note 9 in this chapter).

13. It is enough to go back to *Réflexions* (see chapter 1) to document each of the passages on the "declaration of faith of the friends of blacks."

14. See chapter 2, note 33.

15. Johann Gottfried von Herder, *Another Philosophy of History,* in F. M. Bernard, ed., *On Social and Political Culture* (Cambridge: Cambridge University Press, 1969).

16. "The French Revolution, Slavery and Colonization," was the title of a three-day symposium (February 1989) held in the University of Paris-VIII. This is what can be read in the preface of the conference proceedings: "This is one of the rare meetings, among the numerous conferences of the bicentennial year, to have engaged directly with one of the principal problems of the history of human rights, namely slavery. But neither in its day nor two hundred years later have historians of this great period of our history paid major attention to it." Catherine Coquéry-Vidrovitch, *Esclavage, colonization, libérations nationales: de 1789 à nos jours* (Paris: L'Harmattan, 1990).

17. Speech, cited in note 2 of the preface.

18. *Révolution française et abolition de l'esclavage* (Paris, 1968).

Index

abolitionism, xvi, xxiv
accomplished man (humanity),
  xxii–xxiii, 21
Adorno, T., xxvi. *See also*
  Horkheimer, M.
anthropology, xiii, xxiii, 11, 21,
  23, 46, 69, 78, 80–81, 85, 97,
  104–5
Augustine, Saint, 86, 93, 95–96;
  City of God, 91

Bouckman, 113–15, 122–24,
  126
Buffon, Georges-Louis Leclerc,
  comte de, xxii, 103–6, 110

Christianity, 82, 84
citizenship, xix, xxviii, 60–61,
  63–67, 73, 135, 140, 142

civilizing mission *(mission
  civilisatrice),* xxiii, 56
Code noir, x, xi, xiii, xviii,
  xix, xxv, xxxi, 9, 13, 16, 19,
  33–37, 40, 44, 46, 50–52, 55,
  57, 59, 61–62, 64–66, 69, 73,
  82, 84–85, 104, 109, 114, 116,
  125, 152n3 (intro.), 152n2
  (chap. 1), 152n9, 155n31. *See
  also Spanish Black Code*
Condorcet, J. A. N. de Caritat,
  marquis de, x, xvi, xvii,
  xviii, xix, xxi, xxiii–xxiv,
  xxvii, xxxii, 3, 15, 17–22, 24,
  27–29, 31–32, 34–40, 42–43,
  45–48, 50–52, 68, 75, 85–86,
  98, 109, 119–20, 127–29,
  145–47, 149; *Réflexions sur
  l'esclavage des nègres,* xi, xv,

LOUIS SALA-MOLINS taught political philosophy at the University of Toulouse and at the University of Paris–Sorbonne. His many publications include *Le Code Noir ou le calvaire de Canaan, La Philosophie de l'amour chez Raymond Lulle, Le Dictionnaire des inquisiteurs,* and *La loi, de quel droit?*

JOHN CONTEH-MORGAN teaches French and Francophone studies and African American and African studies at Ohio State University. His publications include *Theatre and Drama in Francophone Africa* and the translation of Paulin Hountondji's *The Struggle for Meaning: Reflections on Philosophy, Culture, and Democracy in Africa.* He is editor of *Research in African Literatures.*